PARTAKERS
of GRACE

PARTAKERS *of* GRACE

A COMMENTARY ON 1 CORINTHIANS

DOUGLAS WILSON

canonpress
Moscow, Idaho

Douglas Wilson, *Partakers of Grace: A Commentary on 1 Corinthians*
Copyright © 2018 by Douglas Wilson

Published by Canon Press
P. O. Box 8729, Moscow, Idaho 83843
800-488-2034 | www.canonpress.com

Cover design by James Engerbretson
Interior design by Valerie Anne Bost
Printed in the United States of America

All rights reserved. No part of this publication may be reproduced, stored in a retrieval system, or transmitted in any form by any means, electronic, mechanical, photocopy, recording, or otherwise, without prior permission of the author, except as provided by USA copyright law.

Unless otherwise indicated, all Scripture quotations are from the King James Version. Bible quotations marked ESV are from the English Standard Version copyright ©2001 by Crossway Bibles, a division of Good News Publishers. Used by permission. Bible quotations marked NKJV are from the New King James Version®. Copyright ©1982 by Thomas Nelson, Inc. Used by permission. All rights reserved.

Library of Congress Cataloging-in-Publication Data is forthcoming.

18 19 20 21 22 23 24 25   10 9 8 7 6 5 4 3 2 1

CONTENTS

INTRODUCTION
1

CHAPTER 1
7

CHAPTER 2
23

CHAPTER 3
33

CHAPTER 4
47

CHAPTER 5
59

CHAPTER 6
67

CHAPTER 7
81

CHAPTER 8
107

CHAPTER 9
117

CHAPTER 10
137

CHAPTER 11
157

CHAPTER 12
185

CHAPTER 13
203

CHAPTER 14
213

CHAPTER 15
231

CHAPTER 16
255

INTRODUCTION

A commonplace among evangelical Christians is the expressed desire to find and join a "New Testament church." For those who have spent any time studying what the conditions on the ground were actually like in the early church, it might be tempting to ask, "What on earth would you want that for?" The Galatians were on the verge of throwing all hope away, being on the edge of falling from grace (Gal. 5:4). The Ephesians had fallen from their first love (Rev. 2:4). Philippi had two of their leading women not on speaking terms (Phil. 4:2).

But Corinth was a special case. There were piles of challenges there. This commentary could even be called *The Basket Case Chronicles* (and in fact, it almost was). If you think that is a bit overstated, we should review some of the issues Paul was having to deal with as he wrote this letter. Some at Corinth were getting drunk at the Lord's Supper (1 Cor. 11:21). There was a guy there who was having sex with his stepmother (1 Cor. 5:1). A number of the other men had to be reminded that the "new members' class" had gone over the necessity of staying away from the pagan prostitutes (1 Cor. 6:15–16). They were suing one another before unbelieving judges (1 Cor. 6:1–8). They were fighting one another over which Bible teacher was the best one (1 Cor. 3:1–7). Do we really want a New Testament church?

At the same time, the apostle Paul loved them deeply, thanking God for them constantly (1 Cor. 1:4). A visit from some of their representatives refreshed him in his spirit (1 Cor. 16:18). He could be greatly moved and affected by their stumbles, but he was no detached critic.

The way the letter is structured is interesting, and reading through it in one sitting is like listening to one half of a phone conversation. The Corinthians had various situations, and a number of questions, which they had sent to Paul. In this letter, Paul appears to be working through the list of questions, answering them methodically. For the most part, we are able to reconstruct what was likely going on in Corinth based on the answers that Paul gives. There are some puzzlers, like the situation in chapter 15 that gets into the baptism for the dead. But generally the letter stands alone in a coherent way without us having access to the original questions.

A review of the problems in Corinth can be disconcerting for modern Christians, ranging from ordinary to outlandish.

Some of their difficulties could be, as far as we are concerned, something that happened five weeks ago instead of two thousand years ago. Christians still sue fellow believers in unbelieving tribunals, for example, thinking nothing of it, but the practice of celibate marriages has not caught on anywhere in the modern church, not even in California.

But for all the problems, Paul had not given up on the Corinthians. And this should perhaps make us want to rethink our approach to "church shopping," where the modern believer treats denominations as though they were malls, with his own role that of an ecclesiastical consumer.

The reason he had not given up on them can be seen when we get to his grand exposition of the resurrection in chapter 15. The message of the gospel is not a like a political campaign, or collecting signatures for a referendum, where if we can only enlist "enough people" then maybe we can get something to happen. Rather, the message we are to preach is that God has set certain inexorable forces in motion, and it is our assigned task to get as many people as prepared as possible before God's great eucatastrophe hits. We are all living along the beach in our miserable little grass huts, and a great tsunami, a huge tidal wave of joy, is heading toward us. Our task is not that of trying to get the tidal wave to come. We cannot make it come any faster, and we most certainly cannot get it to slow down. We declare that it is coming—as the children say, ready or not—and that preparation matters a great deal.

Such preparation includes things like making sure your observances of the Lord's Supper are not occasions of moral disorder. It includes disciplining the man who took his father's wife. It includes settling the disputes within the congregation by remembering that we will judge angels, and so we should be able to sort out the invoices for the failed widget delivery.

It also includes the recognition that this tsunami of joy is not something that will bring joy to all. God's blessings are covenantal, meaning that they are not automatic. He is no vending machine, dispensing goodies blindly. "But with many of them God was not well pleased: for they were overthrown in the wilderness" (1 Cor. 10:5). Those who perished in the wilderness included many who had walked out of Egypt between two walls of water, and no doubt also contained some women who had danced with Miriam beside the sea.

One more important note to consider as you prepare to work through this epistle. The letter is shot through with covenantal realities, and this reality is important to remember when treating historically controversial issues like the Lord's Supper. The partaking that Paul describes when he discusses the Supper is not a partaking that is unique to the Supper. It is not as though the meal is covenantal in a non–covenantal world. No, the world is covenantal, and the covenant with God is represented and sealed in our celebration of the bread and wine. We partake of Christ in the meal, it is true, but the Israelite priests in the Old Testament partook of the sacrifices on the altar, and the pagans partook with demons in their idolatrous services. In other words, partaking in this world is inescapable. It is not whether we partake, but where and how.

One comment should be made about how this book came to be. I send out a weekly exhortation to the saints at Christ Church here in Moscow, an email group mailing called Grace and Peace, and during one stretch of time, I worked through the book of 1 Corinthians, taking just a few verses at a go. When I was done, I just put them all together end to end, with the result that I appear to have been working harder than I was.

DOUGLAS WILSON
March 2018

CHAPTER 1

SAINTS AND SINNERS

> Paul, called to be an apostle of Jesus Christ through the will of God, and Sosthenes our brother, Unto the church of God which is at Corinth, to them that are sanctified in Christ Jesus, called to be saints, with all that in every place call upon the name of Jesus Christ our Lord, both theirs and ours: Grace be unto you, and peace, from God our Father, and from the Lord Jesus Christ. (1 Cor. 1:1–3)

The letter commonly called 1 Corinthians was written by two men—Paul the apostle, and Sosthenes, here simply called "our brother." How much of the letter comes from Sosthenes we don't know, but it was enough to warrant mention (v. 1). Paul identifies himself in accordance with his office as apostle, which was his common practice (v. 1). He was an apostle of Christ through the will of God, which Paul knew full well, recalling how God had called him on the Damascus road. It certainly had not been part of Paul's plans.

This letter was written to the church of God at Corinth (v. 2). This church was made up of those who were *sanctified* in Christ Jesus, and called to be *saints*. These saints had been called alongside everyone who called on the name of Jesus Christ. This Jesus was Lord of the Corinthians, as well as of anyone who called on Him in that same way (v. 2).

Paul pronounces a benediction upon them—grace and peace both, from the Father and from the Son. The Spirit is not mentioned expressly here, but that should not be a great concern. The Spirit *is* the grace and peace that rests upon them (v. 3). Paul has just finished saying that they are sanctified in Christ, and that they are called to be saints. The words used here (for sanctify and saint) are variations on the same word that makes up part of the Holy Spirit's name. So He is not absent at all.

Two other comments. First, Paul is called to be an apostle, and the Corinthians are called to be saints. They are summoned to different stations, but they are both summoned. That summoning occurs in an ongoing way as we call upon the Lord. As we call upon Him, it is revealed that He has indeed called us.

Second, we are going to learn in just a few pages that the Corinthian church had some appalling things going on in it, such that Paul could not identify them as spiritual men, but rather as carnal (3:1–4). Nevertheless, knowing what he is going to say about the state of their sanctification, he still has some high words to say here about the reality of their sanctification. In the same way, we should always stand ready to receive the apostolic rebukes, but we will only be able to do this to the extent that we have heard the apostolic assurances.

GRACE AT CORINTH

> I thank my God always on your behalf, for the grace of God which is given you by Jesus Christ; That in every thing ye are enriched by him, in all utterance, and in all knowledge; Even as the testimony of Christ was confirmed in you: So that ye come behind in no gift; waiting for the coming of our Lord Jesus Christ (1 Cor. 1:4–7)

The next portion of Paul's greeting to the Corinthians should make us think of some things we are going to learn later on in the epistle. Knowing what Paul knew, and knowing what he was going to admonish them for, what he says at the outset is striking. What he says here should not cause us to miss what he says later, but what he says later should not cause us to miss what he says here.

The first thing is that he always thanks God for the grace of God which they had been given (v. 4). The grace was *real*, and the apostle thanked God for it. That grace was also extensive—in *every* thing they were enriched by the Lord, and they had grace in their speech and in their knowledge (v. 5). The testimony of Christ was confirmed in them, and this means that it was a *true* testimony (v. 6). In the matter of spiritual giftedness, they as a church came in second to no one, and they exercised these gifts as they were waiting for the coming of the Lord (v. 7).

There is a tendency among perfectionists to adopt an "all or nothing" approach to this kind of thing. This introductory material is glossed over as so much spiritual boilerplate, and the real status of the church is uncovered when we hear about the man who was living with his stepmother (1 Cor. 5:1), or about the certain members of the church who were getting drunk at the Lord's Supper (1 Cor. 11:21), or about the ones who were taking others of them before unbelieving courts (1 Cor. 6:6). We are all familiar with these (and other) Corinthian failings, and this is why the phrase "basket case" seems to apply. But we should not be so familiar with them that we set aside what Paul says in his greeting here.

He could not address them as spiritual men, but as carnal (1 Cor. 3:1–4). And yet, even though he had to talk to them as though they were carnal, here at the start he assures us that they were anything but carnal. Paul was thankful for the grace of God that was in evidence at Corinth—and so should we be.

TIME WELL SPENT

> Who shall also confirm you unto the end, that ye may be blameless in the day of our Lord Jesus Christ. God

> is faithful, by whom ye were called unto the fellowship of his Son Jesus Christ our Lord. (1 Cor. 1:8–9)

Paul is convinced that God has gotten a good start with the Corinthians—they are equipped and called, and have a solid testimony. And if God begins something, He will finish it. The intent that God has for His people is that they might be blameless in the "day of the Lord Jesus Christ." The Corinthians will finish well because God will confirm them to the end.

Their faithfulness will be the direct result of God's faithfulness. He does not hold onto us because we hold onto Him; it is the other way around. We hold onto Him because He holds onto us. It was "by God" that we were called into the fellowship of His Son, Jesus Christ our Lord, and it is by God that we will be kept in that fellowship. Eternity is not a reward for time well-spent. Time well-spent is the intrusion of eternal grace into our lives here and now.

YOUR KNEES ARE BLIND

> Now I beseech you, brethren, by the name of our Lord Jesus Christ, that ye all speak the same thing, and that there be no divisions among you; but that ye be perfectly joined together in the same mind and in the same judgment. For it hath been declared unto me of you, my brethren, by them which are of the house of Chloe, that there are contentions among you. (1 Cor. 1:10–11)

One of the central problems at Corinth was their fractiousness, and so Paul begins his letter to them by pleading with them, in the name of Jesus Christ, that they drop their contentions. Some from the household of Chloe had told Paul about those contentions, and he saw immediately how destructive they would be (v. 11). He beseeches them, and what he says is quite striking. He asks them to speak the same thing, to avoid divisions in their midst, to be perfectly joined together in the same mind, and to be perfectly joined together in the same judgment (v. 10).

This exhortation is greatly needed in the American church today, not because we invented fractiousness, but because we have sought to make it into a virtue. On the flip side, we have tried to represent obedience to this as a vice. What would we say about a congregation that actually obeyed the apostle's exhortations here? The first thing that would come to mind is that they "had all drunk the Kool-Aid." We would charge the elder board with being a bunch of patsies and yes men.

Of course there *is* a sin associated with mindless conformity—a sin that Paul addresses later in this letter when he demands diversity in the body. The body needs to have different organs—knees, eyes, kidneys. The different organs all perform different functions, and it is not obedience to this passage to try to require the knees to see, or the kidneys to hear. But neither is it obedience to demand that every organ act in a spastic and contrarian way for the sake of the free exchange of ideas. All the organs do different things, but in a body with hand/eye coordination, they do different things *toward the same end*. They should be perfectly joined, which is why Paul pleads for that here.

HOW TIGHT THE BAPTISMAL WAGONS ARE CIRCLED

> Now this I say, that every one of you saith, I am of Paul; and I of Apollos; and I of Cephas; and I of Christ. Is Christ divided? was Paul crucified for you? or were ye baptized in the name of Paul? I thank God that I baptized none of you, but Crispus and Gaius; Lest any should say that I had baptized in mine own name. And I baptized also the household of Stephanas: besides, I know not whether I baptized any other. For Christ sent me not to baptize, but to preach the gospel: not with wisdom of words, lest the cross of Christ should be made of none effect. (1 Cor. 1:12–17)

One of the great problems at Corinth was factionalism and sectarianism and, not surprisingly, false views of baptism were tangled up in the error.

The factionalism was seen in the primary identification that some Christians were putting in the wrong place—"I am of Paul," and so forth (v. 12). Four names are mentioned—Paul, Apollos, Cephas (Peter), and *Christ*. It is interesting to note that the spirit of sectarianism does not vanish simply because the name of Christ is employed. Often that can be the indicator of a hyper-sectarianism—"*I* am of Christ. Not so sure about *you*." So a Christian church can be just as sectarian as a Lutheran or Wesleyan one. Sectarianism is found in the heart and in how tight the baptismal wagons are circled, not on the sign board in front of the church.

Such sectarianism is in evidence when Christ is treated as divided—when anyone who actually belongs to Him is treated as though he does *not* belong to Him. To divide the body is an attempt to divide the Head (v. 13). And if Paul did not die for your sins, still less did Calvin die for them (v. 13). And if no one was baptized in the name of Paul, still less were they baptized in the name of any of the church fathers or reformers. Paul then slides easily from the name into which people were baptized to the person administering at the baptism. He thanks God that he did not actually baptize more than a handful of the Corinthians—Crispus, Gaius (v. 14), and the household of Stephans (v. 16) to be exact. There might have been a few other strays (v. 16), but Paul has established his point. If he had baptized the whole church someone might point to that as evidence that Paul was baptizing in his own name, instead of baptizing Christians into the triune name (v. 15).

Rightly understood, water baptism is certainly a part of the biblical presentation of the gospel (Matt. 28:18–20). But water baptism has been wrongly understood from the very beginning, and so it is important for Paul to distinguish, and sharply, between the heart of what Christ sent him to do, and the external accoutrements of what he had been sent to do. If we get any of this wrong, then the cross of Christ is made of "none effect" (v. 17).

There are two ways this can happen that Paul mentions here. The first is through a wooden sacramentalism which simply collapses baptism and the gospel together. The second is "wisdom of words." If Catholics are prone to the first error, Protestants are to the second. The former have ornate baptismal fonts, the latter ornate pulpits. The human heart will slip off the gospel every chance it gets, and so Paul sets both priestly muttering and pulpiteering arabesques off to the side.

NO EMPTY CROSS

> For the preaching of the cross is to them that perish foolishness; but unto us which are saved it is the power of God. (1 Cor. 1:18)

We will have more to say about this glorious truth in the comments on the verses following, but let's begin with a few observations about the core of this glorious truth.

First, it is not a sign of modern enlightenment for us to discover that "the preaching of the cross" is foolishness to the modern man. It is not foolishness to the new modern man; it is actually foolishness to the *old* man. When people say that preaching the death of Christ is outmoded, they are pretending that there was once a time, back in the day, when it wasn't. But preaching the cross has always been unfashionable. All attempts to make the death of Jesus relevant to death's understanding of life are bound to fail. The only way to make the cross relevant to our old man is to nail that old man to it—which can only be successfully done when the cross is already occupied by our substitute. No sinner was ever saved by an empty cross—an empty tomb, yes, but not an empty cross.

Second, it is foolishness to those who perish. The only way out is for this perishing to perish, for this death to die. This is gospel; this is what gospel *does*. This is its power and authority.

Third, this gospel is incomprehensible to those who need it. This means that in order for anyone to be converted, the efficacy must come from God alone. Sinners recoil from the only thing that can save them—and they have to be saved from that recoil first.

And so last, this passage shows us the absolute necessity of the new birth. There are ultimately two kinds of people in the world—those to whom the cross is foolishness and those to whom it is the power of God. This distinction, at the end of the day, trumps all others.

HIGH PHILOSOPHY ON THE CARPET

> For it is written, I will destroy the wisdom of the wise, and will bring to nothing the understanding of the prudent. Where is the wise? where is the scribe? where is the disputer of this world? hath not God made foolish the wisdom of this world? (1 Cor. 1:19–20)

We should begin with the fact of the taunt, and then move on to the reasons for it. The reasons are given in the verses that follow, but the fact of it is something we too often want to skate around.

When Scripture says that there is a way that "seemeth right unto a man," but "the end thereof are the ways of death" (Prov. 14:12; Prov. 16:25), it is very easy for us to think that Scripture is talking about too much beer or too many red convertibles with blondes in them. You know, *worldly* things. We rarely think of a full scholarship at some Ivy League graduate school, or a very well respected evangelical seminary.

But the world's mainstream doesn't think that lots of cocaine seems right. They do think about wisdom that way, and their scribes that way, and their debaters that way. We really ought to stop imitating the world in that egghead stuff. In the gospel, God takes the world by the back of the neck and rubs our nose in our high philosophy, just like we were a puppy that had piddled on the carpet.

Note the verbs—will destroy, bring to nothing, and made foolish. Wonder what that means. Can't make any sense of it.

THE RIGHT KIND OF IRRELEVANT

> For after that in the wisdom of God the world by wisdom knew not God, it pleased God by the foolishness of preaching to save them that believe. (1 Cor. 1:21)

This does not just say that the world through its wisdom does not know God. It says this inability of the world's wisdom to know God is itself the wisdom of God. It was the wisdom of God that the world by wisdom could not get anywhere. God excluded philosophy as the way to true wisdom (even though the name philosophy means "love of wisdom"). And it is love of wisdom after a sort—the kind of wisdom the world has, and which is incapable of achieving the one thing needful, which is knowledge of God.

Not only did God shut up the way for the smartest guys in the room, but He also opened a way of access by means of preaching. This preaching is foolishness as far as the world is concerned, and always has been. This is why calls to make the preaching of the gospel "relevant" are exercises in vanity. If it is gospel preaching at all, there is no way to make it relevant. What we can hope for instead is that the Spirit of God will move on the preacher, making his declarations the right kind of irrelevant. This is important because just as worldly wisdom cannot attain to the knowledge of God, neither can worldly folly attain to it. Paul is not saying that any old folly will get us there. No, it has to be the folly of *preaching*.

There is folly to man that is also folly to God. There is wisdom to man that is folly to God, and folly to man that is wisdom to God. It is this last one that we need.

TRUE SCANDAL

> For the Jews require a sign, and the Greeks seek after wisdom: But we preach Christ crucified, unto the Jews a stumblingblock, and unto the Greeks foolishness (1 Cor. 1:22–23)

Paul has asked the rhetorical questions—where is the scribe? where is the wise man? where is the great debater? And the implied answer is nowhere. God has made foolish the various worldly ways of being wise. God gave them the folly of preaching when they were looking for something else. Because they were looking elsewhere, they did not come to know God. What were they looking for? Well, at this point Paul lays it out for us.

The Jews, a religious people, with a robust sense of the supernatural, were looking for a *sign*. The Greeks, a philosophically minded people, were seeking after *wisdom*. Instead of those two things, God gave them—through the vehicle of Christ-crucified sermons—a stumblingblock and foolishness respectively. The Jews were walking along looking for a sign in the heavens, and God gave them a stumbling block on the ground, and they fell clean over it. The Greeks were looking for tons of nuance and intellectual sophistication, and God gave them the raging folly of an incarnate Logos, impaled on a gibbet. This is not something Plato could have anticipated.

And God did it on purpose.

COCAINE AND STRIPPERS

> But unto them which are called, both Jews and Greeks, Christ the power of God, and the wisdom of God. Because the foolishness of God is wiser than men; and the weakness of God is stronger than men. (1 Cor. 1:24–25)

Left to themselves, the Jews seek after a sign. Left to themselves, the Greeks pursue what they call wisdom. But fortunately, in the grace of the gospel, the very last thing that God would do is leave us to ourselves. But notice here what God is not leaving us with—He does not abandon us to the sinfulness of seeking supernatural omens, or the stupidity of the philosophy class. When we think of sin, we tend to think of strippers and cocaine, while the apostle Paul thought of images of Jesus appearing in the clouds or the collected works of Aristotle. God's wisdom cannot be made to line up easily with what respectable people believe to be good and wise.

When God is foolish, it is wiser than we are. When God is weak, He is far stronger than we. The reason we are constantly surprised is that not only are we foolish and weak, but we are also very slow learners.

OFFENDING THE CULTURED DESPISERS

> For ye see your calling, brethren, how that not many wise men after the flesh, not many mighty, not many noble, are called: But God hath chosen the foolish things of the world to confound the wise; and God hath chosen the weak things of the world to confound the things which are mighty; and base things of the world, and things which are despised, hath God chosen, yea, and things which are not, to bring to nought things that are: that no flesh should glory in his presence. (1 Cor. 1:26–29)

Paul has just taught us that the wisdom of God is foolishness to man, and that yet the folly of God is wiser than the wisdom of man. We take a statement like this and, if we believe it, we render it safe and unobjectionable by relegating it to some seventeenth dimension in the heavenly places somewhere. Somewhere up there, or way out there, God is thinking thoughts that would be incomprehensible to us if we heard them, and we might be tempted to write it off as folly.

But God's wisdom, that which looks like folly to us, comes down. Just as Christ was Immanuel, God with us, so also He was the wisdom of God—a wisdom that did not look like it (Isa. 53:2). And then, on top of that, when God commissions the messengers of His wisdom, He picks out the unlikeliest ones. And just when we think we have it dialed in—He always picks the losers, we say—He surprises us again. Not *many* wise and mighty, Paul says, not "not *any*."

We measure whether God is at work in the preaching of the cross this way by whether or not the Establishment is confounded. God uses anything at hand—fishermen like James and John, scholars like Saul of Tarsus, ambitious climbers like Augustine, municipal authorities like Ambrose, slave traders like Newton, Anglican priests like Whitefield, and Oxford dons like Lewis. We measure the work by the result. Is flesh abashed? Have we arrived at the result of no flesh trying to glory in the presence of God? Do we preach a flayed Christ, the wisdom of God, nailed to a cross for the sins of the world? Or do we try to make this folly acceptable to the faith's cultured despisers?

WHAT THE GOSPEL HUMILIATES

> But of him are ye in Christ Jesus, who of God is made unto us wisdom, and righteousness, and sanctification, and redemption: that, according as it is written, He that glorieth, let him glory in the Lord. (1 Cor. 1:30–31)

Paul here gets to the bottom line. What is it that insults the wisdom of man? What is it that pushes man's pursuit of signs to the side? What does God do to flummox the philosophers and priests?

God's answer to this is Himself. God gives Himself, and He gives Himself for all that we need. We believers are "in Christ Jesus," and Christ Jesus is the one who is made "unto us" certain things. Christ is given to us as wisdom, and as righteousness, and as sanctification, and as redemption. Christ is all of this to us. Look at it from the other direction. If we have any wisdom, righteousness, sanctification, or redemption that are not found in the person of Jesus Christ, in His life, death, and resurrection, then what we have is not really wisdom, righteousness, sanctification, or redemption.

What is it then? If it is outside Christ, then it is folly, not wisdom. It is evil, not righteousness. It is corrupt, not holy. It is slavery, not redemption. In short, if it glories in anything other than in the Lord, it is the kind of thing that the gospel humiliates.

CHAPTER 2

REMEMBERING THE POINT

> And I, brethren, when I came to you, came not with excellency of speech or of wisdom, declaring unto you the testimony of God. For I determined not to know any thing among you, save Jesus Christ, and him crucified. (1 Cor. 2:1–2)

Paul wanted the message that he preached to be a clear window to the gospel, and not a gaudy, rhetorical mural about the gospel. He wanted the Corinthians to be able to look through what he was saying, and did not want them to stare at what he was saying. In this, he is not rejecting rhetorical wisdom per se, but is actually articulating one of the fundamental principles of wise and judicious rhetoric.

He is saying here that he did not want some florid rhetorical display to get in the way of his listeners' understanding of Jesus Christ, and Him crucified. We sometimes marvel at ingenious television commercials which are witty, sophisticated, and a lot of fun to watch—but which are utter failures because when you are done you can't quite remember what product was being advertised. When that happens, the thing being advertised is actually the wit of the makers of the commercial. When "lengthy prayers in the synagogues" break out, it is because some preacher wants to be on display. When the sermon, like time in the Watts hymn, is "an ever-rolling stream," and it "bears all the congregants away," then that means that somebody is showboating.

NOT JUST BUTTERFLIES

> And I was with you in weakness, and in fear, and in much trembling. And my speech and my preaching was not with enticing words of man's wisdom, but in demonstration of the Spirit and of power: that your faith should not stand in the wisdom of men, but in the power of God. (1 Cor. 2:3–5)

Paul wanted what he preached to have a transforming effect, but he did not want the transformation to be explainable by appeals to a "slick orator." If the success of his preaching was to be grounded on his adherence to the rules of ancient oratory, which was quite refined, then Paul confesses that the whole thing would have been a failure. When Paul got up to speak, he was characterized by weakness, fear, and much trembling. But he is not talking about butterflies before giving a talk at Toastmasters. He is talking about the weight of the message threatening to collapse the rickety cart of his words. There was power there, but the power was much greater than the sum total of power to be found in his eloquence. If it had been any other way, Paul would have been making, not Christians, but Paulinists.

WHAT THEY DID NOT KNOW

> Howbeit we speak wisdom among them that are perfect: yet not the wisdom of this world, nor of the princes of this world, that come to nought: But we speak the wisdom of God in a mystery, even the hidden wisdom, which God ordained before the world unto our glory: Which none of the princes of this world knew: for had they known it, they would not have crucified the Lord of glory. (1 Cor. 2:6–8)

Paul has been telling us that God's folly is wiser than man's wisdom. He then comes to give us the prime example. Paul speaks wisdom among the believers, among those who have been brought to mature perfection. This hidden wisdom is not hidden now, but was rather hidden throughout the course of the Judaic aeon. Now it is revealed; Paul says that "we speak the wisdom of God." God had ordained it before the world was made and had hidden it throughout the course of the world's history before Christ. The princes of this world (the fleshly princelings, and the spiritual forces behind them) did not know what was coming. If they had known, they would not have crucified the Lord of glory—for it was that crucifixion that brought their power down to zero.

Who says that God lacks the wisdom to bring good out of evil? Take the most grotesque murder in the history of the world—what could God possibly do with that? Well, what He did was save the world with it.

WHERE HISTORY IS AIMED

> But as it is written, Eye hath not seen, nor ear heard, neither have entered into the heart of man, the things which God hath prepared for them that love him. But God hath revealed them unto us by his Spirit: for the Spirit searcheth all things, yea, the deep things of God. (1 Cor. 2:9–10)

It is very easy to take the words of verse 9—eye has not seen, ear has not heard—and kick the fulfillment of them "upstairs." Heaven, and the time of the resurrection, is far enough away to enable us to believe things about what it will be like, without actually thinking too much about what it will be like.

But the glories after the resurrection are too distant for this passage. We look at those through a glass darkly, as Paul says later in this book. The apostle John says that it does not yet appear what we shall be like, and yet we long for it. On that subject, the Spirit helps us with groans too deep for words. But here, Paul is talking about something that has been revealed. God has prepared something for the human race, and what He has prepared will come to a glorious fruition in the course of history, prior to the resurrection. And it is that which will stagger the imagination. Eye hasn't seen it yet, and ear has not heard about it, and yet God is in the midst of doing it.

How can we know about it then? God has revealed it to His apostles, by His Spirit, and they wrote it down. There is a glory coming, in which the deep things of God are manifested in human history.

A TRIUNE CONVERSATION

> For what man knoweth the things of a man, save the spirit of man which is in him? Even so the things of God knoweth no man, but the Spirit of God. (1 Cor. 2:11)

The Spirit of God is the interpreter of God, or, as Paul puts it in the previous verse, "the deep things" of God, and here in this verse, "the things" of God. Just as it takes the spirit of a man to interpret his own deepest thoughts, so also it takes the Spirit of God to do the same for the thoughts of God. The Father is the Speaker, the Son is the Spoken, and here we learn that the Spirit is the Interpretation. We as Christians don't have a dry and dusty hermeneutical theory; rather, we worship the Speaker, through His Word, and in the power of His Hermeneutic. We worship a triune and living conversation.

CALCULUS FOR PUPPIES

> Now we have received, not the spirit of the world, but the spirit which is of God; that we might know the things that are freely given to us of God. (1 Cor. 2:12)

The Spirit of God knows what God is up to. The Spirit of God knows the deep things of God. Obviously, the infinite thoughts of the infinite God cannot be given to us—any more than you could teach high level calculus to a puppy not yet housebroken. We cannot contain the deep things of God. But certain aspects of the deep things of God, the things that God has "prepared for them that love him" (v. 9) can be revealed. They were hidden, unrevealed, in previous generations because God had not determined to unveil them yet. So we must distinguish between the secret things that pertain to the nature of God (Dt. 29:29) and the secret things that are only hidden for the time being. The former are incommunicable attributes of God, and cannot be given to creatures. Omniscience cannot be given to a creature, although love can be. Both omniscience and love are attributes of God—and one cannot be shared and the other can be.

One of the things that can be shared with us is what God is going to do for us. The spirit of this world will not tell us these things. The spirit of this world will try to keep this good news away from us. But the Spirit of God, the Holy Spirit, is given to us so that we might know. Know what? The answer is those things that God is giving to us throughout the course of redemptive history. It is the Spirit of God who gives eschatological hope.

HOLY SPIRIT BLUEPRINTS

> Which things also we speak, not in the words which man's wisdom teacheth, but which the Holy Ghost teacheth; comparing spiritual things with spiritual. (1 Cor. 2:13)

The difficulty here is that we often rush to assume what these "spiritual things" might be, and we fill up the content of that category with nice thoughts of observing the Golden Rule, or attending Sunday School regularly, or reviewing your Bible memory verses. But what Paul has been talking about is the future history of the world and the overthrow of all carnality in the running of it. It is true that the logic of the Holy Spirit does not make sense to the natural man (v. 14), even in the details of life. But the reason it does not make sense is because the blueprints the Holy Spirit has drafted for the 23rd century don't make sense to him. Remember that Paul has just told us that eye has not seen, ear has not heard, and the heart has not contemplated, how good God will make that future for those who love Him.

AS IF BY MAGIC

> But the natural man receiveth not the things of the Spirit of God: for they are foolishness unto him: neither can he know them, because they are spiritually discerned. (1 Cor. 2:14)

According the apostle, there are two kinds of men in the world—the natural man and the spiritual man. The natural man is described here as "not receiving" and "not knowing" certain things, the things of the Spirit of God, and the reason he cannot receive or know them is because they are just so much foolishness to him. These things are spiritually discerned, and a natural man has no capacity for spiritual discernment.

This division is important to keep in mind whenever we are talking about the external aspects of the covenant. There are other divisions which we can make in the world as well—baptized and unbaptized, tall and short, rich and poor, and so on. But the most fundamental of all divisions is this division mentioned here, that between the natural and the spiritual man, the unconverted and converted, the unregenerate and regenerate. The Spirit blows where He wills, and we cannot capture Him to make Him do our bidding. We cannot do it with unbiblical antitheses, like race or tribe, and we cannot do it with biblical categories, like baptized and unbaptized.

The presence of this category is made obvious by what we might call Spirit-logic. The Spirit communicates His ways, which results in some receiving them with gladness, and others blinking with no comprehension. When a man is converted, his Bible, as if by magic, turns into English.

THE MIND OF CHRIST

> But he that is spiritual judgeth all things, yet he himself is judged of no man. For who hath known the mind of the Lord, that he may instruct him? But we have the mind of Christ. (1 Cor. 2:15–16)

This is obviously not a blank check, where anyone who claims to be "spiritual" can therefore claim immunity from the judgment of any man. Nevertheless, even though a claim of this kind of spirituality is not sufficient to make the point, the apostle does say that a man who is spiritual sits in judgment on all things, and is himself judged by no one. That Paul considers himself in this category is plain by his claim in the next verse to have "the mind of Christ." We should note also that this includes some other friends of Paul's because he says that "we" have the mind of Christ.

Not having this mind is exhibited by someone pretending to know the mind of the Lord in such a way as to instruct the Lord. In the run-up to this, Paul has been telling us how the Spirit of the Lord is teaching us about the future of the world (vv. 8–10), and so someone who receives this teaching can tell what is going on in the world now. He sits in judgment over all things. To use Jonathan Edwards' illustration, he is in possession of God's blueprints for history, and therefore understands all things from that vantage point. Someone who doesn't have the blueprints is in the position of one who watches the apparent pandemonium of history, and who tries to explain it to God.

To have the mind of Christ is therefore to understand the salvific intent that God has for the whole human race.

CHAPTER 3

STINKY DIAPERS, THEOLOGICALLY SPEAKING

> And I, brethren, could not speak unto you as unto spiritual, but as unto carnal, even as unto babes in Christ. (1 Cor. 3:1)

The apostle Paul has already told us that the Corinthian church was a spiritually gifted church. He said that they came "behind in no gift" (1 Cor. 1:7). They had all the gifts that the Holy Spirit could give, as will become even more evident in his discussion of those gifts later in this book. They had it all—prophecy, tongues, knowledge, the lot. They also had sounding brass and tinkling cymbals.

Here Paul says that they had every gift, and that they were not spiritual, but rather carnal. Spirituality is maturity, not giftedness. Spirituality is measured by the *fruit* of the Spirit, and not by the *gifts* of the Spirit. Love, joy, and peace trump teaching, prophesying, and knowledge.

There are two important lessons here. Sometimes our strict brethren say that such carnal Christians cannot be Christians at all. They say that there are only two possible conditions—spiritual and carnal, and if you are born again you are spiritual, and if you are not you are carnal. Then they brush their hands together. *That* was simple. The problem with that idea is that in this passage, Paul gives "carnal" the appositive of "babes in Christ." Carnality here is certainly *sinful* (1 Cor. 3:3–4), but it is a sinful immaturity in *Christ*. Baby Christians do squabble in the church nursery in unbecoming ways. Christians who are true Christians may be characterized by envying, strife, divisions, party spirit, walking around in the church as though it was supposed to be populated by mere men.

But this leads to the other important lesson. Being a babe in Christ is no compliment. Those who vaunt their gifts, their preacher, their liturgy, their knowledge, their brass and their cymbals, are the red-faced babies in the church nursery, shaking their crib, and throwing toys at the badly instructed infant in the next crib over. Now there *are* those in the church who have not known true conversion. But the presence of stinky diapers is quite possible without that.

ECCLESIASTICAL DRESS-UPS

> I have fed you with milk, and not with meat: for hitherto ye were not able to bear it, neither now are ye able. For ye are yet carnal: for whereas there is among

> you envying, and strife, and division, are ye not carnal, and walk as men? (1 Cor. 3:2–3)

Paul would prefer to teach the Corinthians with "meat," but he was forced by their carnality to stick to milk. They were not yet weaned, which meant they would not be able to bear it if he did give them meat. They were not able in the past, and they are not able now. Not being able to bear true apostolic meat is not the same thing as being unable to bear what some teachers cook up as meat. An adult can savor a thick steak which an infant would think of as impossibly tough and chewy. But the fact that babies find it tough and chewy does not settle the matter. Babies would also find the sole of an old boot tough and chewy.

Notice that Paul speaks of carnality here, but then he does not list what we would normally call *fleshly* sins—lust, fornication, and so on. Carnality in his book is into envy, strife, and division. In the verses that follow, he describes this carnality as swirling around the ankles of two apostles and one Bible teacher, not around cocaine dealers and hookers. Carnality *loves* to do ecclesiastical dress-ups.

But again, this carnality does not mean they are not Christians. This carnality is truly sinful, but it characteristic of "babes in Christ" (v. 1).

AN ARCHED EYEBROW PROBLEM

> For while one saith, I am of Paul; and another, I am of Apollos; are ye not carnal? Who then is Paul, and who is Apollos, but ministers by whom ye believed, even as

> the Lord gave to every man? I have planted, Apollos watered; but God gave the increase. So then neither is he that planteth any thing, neither he that watereth; but God that giveth the increase. (1 Cor. 3:4–7)

Spiritual growth is a mysterious thing, one that comes directly from the hand of God. Paul here distinguishes instruments or means of grace, and the grace itself. The ministers of the gospel proclaim it, the teachers of the Word nurture the newly planted seed, but only the direct and gracious intervention of God causes anything actually to happen. To latch onto the external instruments (which God does use) is to be carnal.

Paul has already defined this carnality as both sinful and as spiritually infantile. Jacob and Esau hear the same word, but they respond differently. Two men receive water from the same baptismal font, from the hands of the same minister, but one goes to Heaven and the other to Hell. Two men go in very different directions, and this is because God gave the increase in the one instance and not in the other. This is in conjunction with His appointed means, not independent of them, but they are not so conjoined as to make them work automatically apart from His blessing. His blessing is therefore a direct and immediate blessing.

We also cannot let this passage pass by noting that a wrong-headed attachment to strong personalities is nothing new in the Church, and that Paul dismisses it as a phenomenon worthy of the ecclesiastical nursery. This is the Pauline doctrine. It is also the Apollonian. Note also that a man cannot escape from the spirit of infantile sectarianism by describing himself as merely a "Christian." Those guys were the worst (1 Cor. 1:12). Sectarianism is a heart problem: an arched eyebrow problem, not a label problem.

ONE PURPOSE

> Now he that planteth and he that watereth are one: and every man shall receive his own reward according to his own labour. For we are labourers together with God; ye are God's husbandry: ye are God's building. (1 Cor. 3:8–9)

At the end of this passage, Paul shifts the metaphor from one of agriculture to one of architecture. But before he makes that shift, he makes it clear that different ministers with differing spiritual gifts, or with different roles to play in the history of those they minister to, are part of the same team. One man plants, and another man waters, and these two men are one—they labor to one purpose. If the first had not planted, there would be nothing to water. If the second did not water, there was no sense in planting.

So as far as these two laborers are concerned, they are functioning as a unit, and the point of unity is God Himself. Paul and Apollos were laborers together with God. God plants through the one who plants, and God waters through the one who waters. For the two laborers to compete is an attempt to get God to compete with Himself, which He will not do.

At the same time, the fact that the two ministers are one in purpose and intent does not mean that God is incapable of keeping track of what they do. God does this—but they should not. Each person who labors in this field will receive his own reward, and it will be in accordance with his own work. But God is the only one who really knows the value of the labor of each, and so we leave this in His hands.

Whenever a Christian grows, it is God's husbandry. Whenever a Christian is edified and built up, it is God's construction.

AND POOF, IT WAS GONE

> According to the grace of God which is given unto me, as a wise masterbuilder, I have laid the foundation, and another buildeth thereon. But let every man take heed how he buildeth thereupon. For other foundation can no man lay than that is laid, which is Jesus Christ. (1 Cor. 3:10–11)

The word here for master builder is the word from which we get *architect*. And Paul describes himself not just as a kind of builder, but as a wise one. This is the passage that sets up the famous description in the next few verses about the person who makes it into Heaven with his coat tails burning—but the import of this is often missed. Those verses are not talking, in the first instance, about an average Christian living an average Christian life, but rather talking about *ministers* and *ministries*. Some ministries withstand the fire, and are glorified in it. Others are consumed, although the minister himself is saved. Billy Bob is in glory, but Billy Bob's Worldwide Global Outreach . . . isn't. *Poof*, and it was just gone.

The essential thing that a master builder must remember here has two aspects. The first is that he must not build where there is no foundation, or try to substitute some other foundation (v. 11). The second, made more evident in the following section, is that the materials used to build upon Christ must be the right kind of material. The master builder must build *in line with* the existing foundation, which is Christ, and he must build with material that is consistent with that foundation. Excellent materials must not be erected in a bog, with no foundation beneath, and pathetic materials must not be used on an excellent foundation.

AND THE CHILDREN YOU HAVE GIVEN ME

> Now if any man build upon this foundation gold, silver, precious stones, wood, hay, stubble; Every man's work shall be made manifest: for the day shall declare it, because it shall be revealed by fire; and the fire shall try every man's work of what sort it is. If any man's work abide which he hath built thereupon, he shall receive a reward. If any man's work shall be burned, he shall suffer loss: but he himself shall be saved; yet so as by fire. (1 Cor. 3:12–15)

There are several reasons why the apostle Paul is not talking about Purgatory here. First, we are talking about ministers and their ministries, not Christians and their venial sins. Second, this happens instantaneously—the *day* shall declare it. The fire involved is testing the permanence of a man's work and ministry, and not the state of his soul. And last, the minister concerned is saved instantaneously on that day of revelation, but he suffers the loss of not being able to take the fruit of his ministry with him into glory.

Paul says that the faithful minister, by way of contrast, "shall receive a reward." What kind of reward might that be? The apostle is not thinking of anything so crass as a chest of heavenly doubloons. The rewards of glory are commensurate with the rewards of the ministry itself. The rewards are consistent with the attitudes that attained to the reward (1 Thess. 2:19–20). So what does that mean? What is Paul's crown? His hope? What is his glory and joy? He tells the Thessalonians . . . is it not *you*? The gold and silver and precious stones that are built on this foundation of Jesus Christ are eternal souls. Wood, hay and stubble are ratings, website hits, popularity, trendy relevance, blurbs from important scribes . . . and lost eternal souls.

Later on, Paul tells these same Corinthian Christians that their labor in the Lord is not in vain (1 Cor. 15:58). Here we see that there is a kind of labor which is performed in this life, the effects of which carry over into the next. There are two areas where every minister should invest all that he has. What lasts forever? What stretches across the eschaton, with one end in the ministry of today and the other end in glory? I can think of two things that should be considered. The first is Scripture—the grass withers, the flower fades, but the Word of the Lord endures forever (1 Pet. 1:24–25). The second is your neighbor. Every faithful minister should yearn to be able to echo the words of the Lord Jesus when he finally appears before God . . . here am I, and the children you have given me (Heb. 2:13).

A LIVING TEMPLE

> Know ye not that ye are the temple of God, and that the Spirit of God dwelleth in you? (1 Cor. 3:16)

Paul here uses an image he will return to later in this letter. What is striking here is that he is describing the temple of God as being made up of these Christians corporately. He uses the plural—you, all of you together, make up the one temple of God. This temple has been consecrated by the Spirit of God who dwells in our corporate midst. In other words, individual Christians are individual bricks, stones, and pillars—or, returning to his earlier example, gold, silver, or precious stones. To take the image that Peter uses, these stones are alive; they are living stones. The temple is made up of living gold, living silver, and living jewels.

There are two aspects of this that a wise master builder should pay attention to. First, he should not seek to build with the wood, hay, and stubble of dead *things*. There are ways to measure success that the world uses that have nothing to do with how God measures it. Fame, buildings, wealth, and so on look permanent to some people, but they are just so much smoke. Do not build a ministry out of dead things. But the second aspect of this is that we should not seek to build a ministry out of dead people either. The Word of God constantly points to the absolute necessity of the new birth. How could the Spirit of life possibly indwell a house made out of dead souls? He is the Spirit of *life*.

JOGGING CORINTHIANS

> If any man defile the temple of God, him shall God destroy; for the temple of God is holy, which temple ye are. (1 Cor. 3:17)

In Paul's argument, this kind of defilement is brought about by sexual sin, and only by sexual sin. A few chapters later, when he tells the Corinthians to flee from fornication (1 Cor. 6:18), he says that every other sin is "without the body." But the one who commits sexual uncleanness is the one who sins against his own body, which is the temple of the Holy Spirit (1 Cor. 6:19). And so this exhortation is not about doing the right number of sit ups in the morning, or avoiding refined sugar. The idea of urging the Corinthians to take up jogging never came into Paul's head.

Of course, there are good stewardship arguments that can be marshaled against the practice of giving yourself lung cancer, or bungee jumping with frayed cords, or hitting your splayed fingers with a hammer. It is possible (and easy) to sin against God through foolish stewardship. But such poor stewardship sins do not create the kind of defilement that Paul is addressing here.

It is worth noting that we are not just told that this defilement is something that God is "against." We are explicitly told that God will undertake to destroy the one who does this. All of a sudden, cruising porn sites is not nearly as compelling as it once was.

SELF-DECEIVED

> Let no man deceive himself. If any man among you seemeth to be wise in this world, let him become a fool, that he may be wise. For the wisdom of this world is foolishness with God. For it is written, He taketh the wise in their own craftiness (1 Cor. 3:18–19)

In Paul's discussion here, the concepts of wisdom and folly extend past these two verses. But we should begin with a few introductory comments about it that can be seen here.

The first is the danger of self-deception. How is it possible for a man to tell lies to himself, *and* to believe them? How can a man be simultaneously both liar and deceived? It seems emotionally complicated, but it is clearly possible. One place where this happens is when people hear the Bible taught, but don't do it. They think that Bible listening is the same thing as Bible doing (Jas. 1:22). They wouldn't put up with such sermons, or so they think, if they weren't doing them.

This passage makes it clear that another place where we deceive ourselves is in regard to the question of what constitutes true wisdom. When the whole world acclaims you as a wise man, there ought to be a deep, reflexive *uh oh*. In this case a man is self-deceived when he listens to what the whole world says about him. It is called *self*-deception because the reason the world's flattery made sense to him is that he had been flattering himself first. This particular cob of corn was previously buttered.

A man in this position should do something foolish. In context, this means foolish in the eyes of the world, so that he might actually become wise (in the eyes of God). God thinks that this world's string of awards, degrees, accolades, and lifetime achievement medals are stupid. Moreover, He allows men to fall into the trap of unbelief caused by such things. And it *is* unbelief. How can you believe, Jesus asks, as long as you accept honor from one another (John 5:44)? This propensity to this kind of self-deception is a trap that God uses to catch the crafty and self-important.

Of course, careful cross-referencing will show that the quotation in verse 19 is from the book of Job, and it is from one of Job's false comforters, Eliphaz the Temanite. Though the words are true, Eliphaz himself was one of those caught in just this way, in fulfillment of his own words.

A CROW THAT STRUTS IN THE GUTTER

> And again, The Lord knoweth the thoughts of the wise, that they are vain. Therefore let no man glory in men. For all things are yours; Whether Paul, or Apollos, or Cephas, or the world, or life, or death, or things present, or things to come; all are yours; And ye are Christ's; and Christ is God's. (1 Cor. 3:20–23)

In the previous verse, Paul had quoted from the book of Job. Here he quotes from Psalm 94:11, and to the same effect. God knows that the thoughts of the world's wise men are vain. God knows that their thoughts are *futile*. The context of that psalm has to do with the insolence of how proud men rule—and this would include how they rule the bastions of higher learning. God will recompense the proud (Ps. 94:2), even if they have been glorying in their wickedness for a long time (Ps. 94:3). A throne of iniquity cannot have fellowship with God (Ps. 94:20), and we may by extension apply this to endowed chairs.

When Paul says that we ought not therefore to glory in men, he is talking about men's ways of reckoning wisdom, whenever God in His judgment leaves them to their own devices. Worldliness is an attitude, and not a function of materiality. The material world was made by God. Worldliness was crafted in the hearts of men.

We should then note how Paul's reasoning works, and we can best do this by working up from his conclusion. Christ belongs to God. We belong to Christ. And absolutely everything in the world belongs to us. This means that absolutely everything, through man, through Christ, belongs to God. Paul is careful to push this into all the corners. What belongs to the believers, who are the inheritance of Christ, who is the inheritance of God? Apostles and Bible teachers belong to the saints. The world belongs to them (after they have thrown away the vanity of wise men). Life and death belong to them. We would also include things right now, and things to come. Everything is yours, Paul says. Why would someone who stands to inherit that kind of wealth envy the pretensions of the scholars of this world? A king on a balcony of his palace does not look down on the street below in order to envy the crow that struts in the gutter.

CHAPTER 4

ROWING UNDER

> Let a man so account of us, as of the ministers of Christ, and stewards of the mysteries of God. Moreover it is required in stewards, that a man be found faithful. (1 Cor. 4:1–2)

Paul then describes himself, and those with him, under two different headings. The first is that of a minister, and the second that of a steward. These men were ministers of Christ, and stewards of the mysteries of God.

The word *minister* here is *huperetes*, a compound of the word for "under" and the word for "rowing"—the kind of situation that used to result from ships having two or three banks of oars. An under-rower would work at the direction of another, which in this case would be Christ. John Mark once labored in this capacity for Barnabas and Saul (Acts 13:5). We would call someone like this an assistant pastor. Paul wants men to account of him this way, to reckon him as a servant of Christ, laboring under the direct authority of Christ.

The word for *steward* is *oikonomos*, and refers to a manager of the household affairs, a chamberlain. He must direct and manage, and he must also be able to give an accounting for all the silver. He is entrusted with certain responsibilities, and he must be found faithful in his discharge of his duties. Pastors are here described as stewards, but of what? The answer is something much more valuable than the household jewels, or the receivables and payables. Ministers of Christ are stewards of the mysteries of God. This refers to the gospel, that which unites Jew and Gentile, heaven and earth, and God and man. There must be no tampering with this gospel, either by adding or subtracting. Just the ancient gospel, straight up.

PRAISE OF GOD

> But with me it is a very small thing that I should be judged of you, or of man's judgment: yea, I judge not mine own self. For I know nothing by myself; yet am I not hereby justified: but he that judgeth me is the Lord. Therefore judge nothing before the time, until the Lord come, who both will bring to light the hidden things of darkness, and will make manifest the counsels of the hearts: and then shall every man have praise of God. (1 Cor. 4:3–5)

Paul has just finished explaining that he labors as a steward, a person who must give an accounting of his work to the one who commissioned him. But he does not have to give an accounting of his heart to the other stewards. This is why Paul says that it is a trifle with him (a very small thing) if he is judged by the Corinthians, or by any other man for that matter (v. 3). In fact, Paul labors as one who will give an account, but he does not try to weigh the accounts himself. He does not even judge himself (v. 3).

His conscience is clear, but that does not mean he is justified. The one who judges in these matters is the Lord. A man's conscience is a good rule of thumb to be obeyed, but it is by no means absolute. A man's conscience can be clear and yet he is still guilty before God (v. 4)—a truth that ought to be meditated upon more than it is.

Paul says that judgments should not be rendered before the time, that time being when the Lord comes and settles all accounts. He will do this by bringing hidden things out of the darkness, and He will haul the counsels of our hearts out into the clear light of day. He will make them manifest. But Paul ends with a surprising twist. He does not end this thought by saying that we will all then be seen as guilty wretches—no, he is speaking of stewards who have been laboring as ones who must give an account. And at that day "every man" shall have "praise of God." When God settles all accounts at the end of the world, He will not just condemn. There will no doubt be some surprising condemnations (1 Cor. 3:15). Although none of this can happen outside of Jesus Christ, Paul here points to a surprising number of *vindications*. How else can we take "praise of God"?

BEYOND WHAT IS WRITTEN

> And these things, brethren, I have in a figure transferred to myself and to Apollos for your sakes; that ye might learn in us not to think of men above that which is written, that no one of you be puffed up for one against another. (1 Cor. 4:6)

Paul here is talking about the universal tendency that Christians have to take pride in their teachers. In the first century, they were lining up behind Paul and Apollos (and Cephas and Christ), and they were doing so with a factional party spirit.

In the first verse of this chapter, Paul was talking about ministers and stewards of the gospel of God. Here he is doing the same. We have a good basis therefore for believing that the intermediate material is also about judging ministers. He is not talking in the first instance about judging himself morally or ethically (vv. 3–4), but rather about judging his effectiveness as a teacher of Scripture. Paul tells us explicitly in verse 6 that what he has been writing he is applying to himself and to Apollos for their sakes.

He urges them not to go beyond what is written. This can be applied in two ways. First, we should not value our teachers more highly than the Bible says to. We are to honor them, and we should not fall short in this duty, but we must also remember that one form of dishonor is to idolize them. So, we should think of our teachers the way in which we are instructed by Scripture to think of them.

Second, we should beware of showboating hermeneutics. If a man is painting exegetical filigrees up by the ceiling fans in the sanctuary, then it is probably being done to draw attention to himself. "Going beyond what is written" is a good way for him to emphasize the kind of "distinctives" that get people coming to his church. When that happens, congregants get puffed up for their teacher over against the other guy's teacher. Then, when the other guy gets more successfully puffed up, the losing puffer can become deflated and discouraged. He reluctantly (and with grief in his heart) concludes that he is "not getting fed" any more, and heads down the road.

WE THINK WE HIT A TRIPLE

> For who maketh thee to differ from another? and what hast thou that thou didst not receive? now if thou didst receive it, why dost thou glory, as if thou hadst not received it? (1 Cor. 4:7)

The context here is that of boasting in your Bible teachers, whether Luther, or Calvin, or any other valued servant of God. In the backdrop is this: if it is bad teaching, why boast in it? If it is good teaching, then it is a gift, and this means that you ought not to boast in it either. If you were given a bad thing, don't boast—it is *bad*. If you were given a good thing, don't boast—it was *given*.

Paul is here identifying a particular way in which Christians give way to vainglory. He says that they glory in what they have been taught, and this glory is a false glory that acts as though they did not receive it as a gift. Calvinists are the worst when they fall into this, because there are multiple layers of irony involved. They say that they alone among Christians teach that no glory can accrue to the creature, and that all glory must go to the Creator alone. Having said this, they glory in the fact that they said it.

Now the particular instance of this principle that Paul applies has to do with teachers of Scripture. But the principle applies across the board—it applies everywhere God gives gifts, and that of course is everywhere. How can you boast in your blue eyes, in your intelligence, in your height, in your race or ethnicity, in your birth place, in your birth order, in your attractiveness, or in the shape of your nose? What do you have that wasn't a present? Way too many of us were born on third base and we think we hit a triple.

THEIR RAGGEDY FOUNDER

> Now ye are full, now ye are rich, ye have reigned as kings without us: and I would to God ye did reign, that we also might reign with you. (1 Cor. 4:8)

Paul is about to explain to the Corinthians the apostolic spectacle in which he was a participant, and he sets this explanation up by telling us how rapidly the desire for respectability sets in once a church has been established for more than ten minutes. A church is planted by a visionary, by a pioneer, by an unreasonable man. It couldn't be done, everyone said, until the unreasonable man did it. But then, after a requisite amount of time goes by, the urbane sophisticates that now populate this church become a little embarrassed of their raggedy founder.

This is the phenomenon that happened at Corinth. *Now* they were full. *Now* they were rich. *Now* they reigned as kings "without" the apostles. But of course, this is all going on inside their heads and only there—they are not really reigning. Paul actually wishes that they were ready for the maturity of godly rule, for if that were the case, then the apostles might be allowed to join them. But the kind of maturity that "outgrows" the zeal of the founders is actually a deformation, and not a maturation at all.

APOSTLES ARE TROUBLESOME WHEN ALIVE

> For I think that God hath set forth us the apostles last, as it were appointed to death: for we are made a spectacle unto the world, and to angels, and to men. We are fools for Christ's sake, but ye are wise in Christ; we are weak, but ye are strong; ye are honourable, but we are despised. (1 Cor. 4:9–10)

Apostles are very honored in retrospect, which is safe to do now that they are all dead. Have we not built their memorials? Do we not have impressive churches with St. in front of Paul and Peter? Ah, but a *living* apostle would have trouble getting a call to be a pastor in such a church. Too much jail time on his resume.

This is all by God's appointment. Men who have taken up a cross are men who overcome the world. They bring up the rear, and in fulfillment of Christ's words, we find that they are first of all. They are a *spectacle* to the world, and to angels, and to men. Paul points out the disparity between the apostles and the church in Corinth—the apostles are fools, but they are wise. The apostles are weak, but they are strong. The Corinthians are honorable, but the apostles are despised. Paul didn't use scare quotes, but if he did, they would be around "wise," "strong," and "honorable." In the very next chapter, we find that one of them had his father's wife. In the next chapter after that, we find that some of them are screeching at each other in the courts of the unbelievers. In that same chapter, some of the Corinthian men had to have it explained to them that Christian men don't get to visit the sacral prostitutes. Their worship services were bedlam. Wise, strong, and honorable, aye.

But this means that it must be possible for professing Christians to behave in a despicable manner, and yet without forfeiting the kind of honor that the world bestows. Let us not wonder at this because there are probably hundreds of examples of it within a twenty-mile radius of your house.

GREASE IN THE DUMPSTER

> Even unto this present hour we both hunger, and thirst, and are naked, and are buffeted, and have no certain dwellingplace; And labour, working with our own hands: being reviled, we bless; being persecuted, we suffer it: Being defamed, we intreat: we are made as the filth of the world, and are the offscouring of all things unto this day. I write not these things to shame you, but as my beloved sons I warn you. (1 Cor. 4:11–14)

This passage connects tightly to the verses that follow, and so we have to remember the context. Paul goes on to urge the Corinthians to imitate him as a father (vv. 15–16). But the context of that following exhortation is set here. This is not a bourgeois father exhorting a ne'er-do-well son. This is a father who is under various forms of unjustified disgrace, who is warning his sons against the dangers of respectability.

Apostles, and by extension visionary leaders and founders, are the kind of people who have a thick layer of respectability imputed to them, such that the actual sacrifices they are making and the stands they are taking are invisible to those who are building up their own reputations on the foundation of these apostles and prophets. Paul here cites contempt, physical challenges, financial challenges, persecution, and the fact that they are the "offscouring" of all things, right up to the present. The apostolic glory is that of being grease in the dumpster out back of the restaurant.

Note and mark the danger well. The danger is creeping respectability. It is the way of all flesh. This temptation always arises. The third generation builds a grand brick library on the campus of a college founded by a man who spent a great deal of his ministry making fun of books, and the pointy-headed scholars who shuffled around carrying them, in order to cite them to one another.

Paul is not feeling sorry for himself here. He is pointing out something that should have been glaringly obvious to people who had a moral obligation to have seen it already, and whose inability to see it was a great spiritual danger to them. The apostolic band that Paul was the center of labored under unbelievable opprobrium. Moreover, they were able to do this without their "beloved sons" even noticing it. Paul therefore *warns* them. Take heed. If you must have great learning, as Paul most certainly did, make sure to carry it in such a way as to make people think you are crazy (Acts 26:24). It is the only safe way.

NOW THAT'S PAULINE

> For though ye have ten thousand instructors in Christ, yet have ye not many fathers: for in Christ Jesus I have begotten you through the gospel. Wherefore I beseech you, be ye followers of me. (1 Cor. 4:15–16)

Remember that Paul is talking about the contrast between the disreputable condition of being an apostle (v. 9) and the faux respectability of churches founded by those same apostles (v. 8). He is talking about the tendency that Christians have to distance themselves from the kind of people that God used to establish them in the first place. This is not a modern phenomenon; it is how worldliness counterattacks whenever God does a remarkable work of grace.

Paul's antidote for this is godly imitation. He is their father, and while they may have learned lots of things from ten thousand books at the ivy-covered library down at the seminary, they don't have that many fathers. Therefore, he begs them to follow him. Imitate him. In what? Well, he wants them to imitate him in what he is talking about—a willingness to be talked about, laughed at, called a discredit to the gospel, and snorted over in the faculty lounge.

Every Christian scholar and pastor needs to make this a personal life goal. We need to learn to live in what one Puritan called the "high mountain air of public calumny." Now *that's* Pauline.

CHRISTIAN COPIES

> For this cause have I sent unto you Timotheus, who is my beloved son, and faithful in the Lord, who shall bring you into remembrance of my ways which be in Christ, as I teach every where in every church (1 Cor. 4:17)

In the verse prior, Paul begged the Corinthians to "follow" him. The word for *follow* there is the word we get *mimetic* from—he is talking about imitation. In the verse prior to that he identifies himself as more than a teacher. He was their father. The way children follow a father is by means of imitation. As dearly loved children, Paul says elsewhere, be imitators of God (Eph. 5:1). Children imitate.

Now in this verse, we learn that imitation can work at a distance. Timothy was a dearly loved son to Paul, and he sent Timothy to be with the Corinthians so that they could see Paul's reflection in him. As a beloved son, he had imitated Paul. Paul knew this—he was "faithful in the Lord." Consequently he was in a position to remind them of Paul's way of life, and Paul's way of life was something he taught in all the churches.

The Christian life is a *way*, and it is a way that must be *copied* if we are to understand it rightly.

KINGDOM HORSEPOWER

> Now some are puffed up, as though I would not come to you. But I will come to you shortly, if the Lord will, and will know, not the speech of them which are puffed up, but the power. For the kingdom of God is

> not in word, but in power. What will ye? shall I come unto you with a rod, or in love, and in the spirit of meekness? (1 Cor. 4:18–21)

The apostle now mentions some at Corinth who would cast themselves in the role of his opponents. They talk as though Paul *talks* big, but he isn't going to come here. But Paul says that he will in fact come, if God allows it, and these wiseacres will find out that Paul is not puffed up like they are. He will come with power—the kingdom is in power, and not mere words. What would you rather, Paul asks. Should Paul come with a rod, or with love and meekness?

In 1 Corinthians 13, a few chapters down the road, Paul contrasts the word translated "puffed up" with love. Here he contrasts it with power. There it is arrogant, and does not act lovingly. Here it is arrogant, and cannot follow through on its boastful claims.

Paul will indeed come, and he will check out the boastful claims of these puffer birds, and he will see how far they can fly in that condition. The kingdom of God, Paul says, is potent. He therefore asks the Corinthians what they would prefer. Would they like love that disciplines, as with a rod, or love that seems more like love, in a spirit of meekness? But either way the power is there.

CHAPTER 5

MORE LIKE THE GENTILES

> It is reported commonly that there is fornication among you, and such fornication as is not so much as named among the Gentiles, that one should have his father's wife. And ye are puffed up, and have not rather mourned, that he that hath done this deed might be taken away from among you. (1 Cor. 5:1–2)

Paul now begins to discuss particular problems that he had heard were afflicting the church at Corinth. This particular outrage—a man in a sexual relationship with his stepmother—had two sides to the problem. The first was that it had happened at all. The second was the attitude that the Corinthians had toward it. They somehow thought it was a badge of their insight—they were puffed up over this. If they had really been wise, they would have mourned, and they would have copied the Gentiles in their rejection of the perversion. Paul is saying, "Why can't you be more like the non-Christians here?"

The man who had done this thing needed to be removed from the Church. The fact that he had not been removed means that the Corinthians had mistaken the nature of grace. Grace does not allow us to live at a lower level than the pagans—"Christians aren't perfect, just forgiven," as our bumper stickers have it. Grace lifts us up, but abuses of grace plunge us deeper than even the heathen will go. Common grace does not do what uncommon grace does, what special grace does, but it does far more than twisted grace. So the answer to twisted grace is church discipline, a practice that helps Christians learn how to be more hard-headed. Like the Gentiles.

JUDGMENT FROM A DISTANCE

> For I verily, as absent in body, but present in spirit, have judged already, as though I were present, concerning him that hath so done this deed (1 Cor. 5:3)

Paul is referring to the man in the previous verses who was in a sexual relationship with his stepmother, something which even the Gentiles wouldn't approve. Paul is willing to judge the case from a distance, and he is clearly doing this because the facts of the case were not in dispute. If a man were charged with having a sexual relationship with his stepmother, but denied it, and someone from a distance made a judgment without hearing all sides, this would be a travesty of justice (Prov. 18:17).

But this is "reported commonly" (v. 1), and the Corinthians were puffed up over their display of grace. In other words, Paul is making a judgment about the false Corinthian view of grace, in response to a public disgraceful fact, and is fully within his rights to do so. Because he represents the truth in this matter, his physical absence doesn't matter. His words in this letter convey the authority of his spirit.

As a passing comment, we should note that the man involved in this sin is not necessarily the same man that is referred to in 2 Cor. 2:5–11.

HIS NAME AND HIS POWER

> In the name of our Lord Jesus Christ, when ye are gathered together, and my spirit, with the power of our Lord Jesus Christ, To deliver such an one unto Satan for the destruction of the flesh, that the spirit may be saved in the day of the Lord Jesus. (1 Cor. 5:4–5)

Paul requires the Corinthian church to gather together in order to expel the wicked man from their midst. Later he calls this not "keeping company" (v. 11), and he says that they are to "put away" such a wicked person (v. 13). This is called a purgation (v. 7). In the verses to come we will consider why Paul had to exhort them this way, but for now, we need to simply look at *what* he tells them to do.

He says that they are to declare this sentence of discipline in the assembly, when they are gathered together. Church discipline, when it gets to this point, should be public. He says that it is to be done in the name of the Lord Jesus, which in this instance Paul equates with being done with the power of the Lord Jesus. His name and His power accompany one another.

The discipline has the eventual salvation of the one disciplined in view, but recognizes that it will go hard with him in the meantime. His flesh (that which he was serving idolatrously) was going to be destroyed, and it was going to be destroyed by Satan, the accuser. Satan is nothing if not a prosecutor. After he has enticed a man with his father's wife, suggesting that it would be a fine opportunity, there is nothing to keep him from turning immediately to accusation once the deed is done. And when a man is put out of the Church, this removes him from the availability of our Advocate, our Defense Attorney (1 John 2:1). A man outside the Church has to fend off the accusations all by himself, which is impossible to do.

A TRIUMPH OF GRACE, OR SOMETHING

> Your glorying is not good. Know ye not that a little leaven leaveneth the whole lump? Purge out therefore the old leaven, that ye may be a new lump, as ye are unleavened. For even Christ our passover is sacrificed for us (1 Cor. 5:6–7)

The Corinthians were not putting up with this guy who had his father's wife, feeling a little sheepish or guilty about it. They thought their attitude toward him was a triumph of grace, or something. They were *glorying* in how their attitude was handling a difficult situation for all.

Paul says, in effect, that certain sins *grow*. A little leaven affects the whole loaf. In this instance, the leaven is tolerated sin, of a kind which can only grow and get worse. Church discipline in such a case is not only zeal for the holiness of God, but it is also an act of self-defense. When such sins are considered tolerable, the Church becomes a breeding ground for such things.

In the next breath, Paul says that Christ was our Passover, sacrificed "for us." In the original Passover story, the Passover lamb was killed, and because of this, the angel of death would "pass over" any house with that blood on the doorposts. To tolerate sin in the Church is to refuse to eat the unleavened bread, which is to not keep the Passover, which is to not have the blood on the doorposts, and which leaves you as exposed as the Egyptians were.

THE LEAVEN OF MALICE

> Therefore let us keep the feast, not with old leaven, neither with the leaven of malice and wickedness; but with the unleavened bread of sincerity and truth. (1 Cor. 5:8)

Christians celebrate Passover. In this passage, they do so through recognition of three things. The first is that Christ was *the* Pascal lamb, sacrificed for us. The second is the rejection of the *old* leaven, the kind of typological leaven that the old covenant saints would banish from their homes annually. We do not keep the feast that way. We have banished the annual rite of ritual leaven banishment. And the third is another image—leaven here representing, not a God-given pattern of behavior in the Old Testament, but rather the yeast of human sinfulness. The two aspects of this sinfulness that are mentioned in particular are malice and wickedness. They are contrasted with sincerity and truth, making the parallel point that the malice is hypocritical and insincere and the wickedness is based, as wickedness must be, on falsehood. Believers are called, in this sense, to celebrate Passover constantly. There is never a time when malice and wickedness can be allowed into our homes. There is never a time when we can return to the old covenant ways—not because there was too much Passover there, but because there was not enough. We needed 364 more days of it. And there is never a time when Christ was not slain for us.

LEAVING THE PLANET

> I wrote unto you in an epistle not to company with fornicators: Yet not altogether with the fornicators of this world, or with the covetous, or extortioners, or with idolaters; for then must ye needs go out of the world. (1 Cor. 5:9–10)

Paul had written an epistle to the Corinthians previously (which means that 1 Corinthians is actually 2 Corinthians), and in this letter he had told them that they were not to hang out with fornicators. But this can be misunderstood, and Paul writes here to head off such a misunderstanding. He did not mean to prohibit Christians from associating with fornicators—the intention was to keep Christians from associating with fornicators who called themselves

Christians (as we will see in the next verse). The same thing applies to covetous people, and swindlers, and idolaters. It is *fine* to have lunch with such people. To avoid that kind of contact you would have to leave the planet, which Paul is not asking for.

It is more than a little interesting that when the Church refuses to practice church discipline, this Pauline assumption gets inverted. Paul says that we can hang out with non-Christians who live like this, but not with professing Christians who do. But when the Church doesn't discipline, Christians hang out with professing Christians who are immoral and dishonest (sitting across from them at the potluck), and they do not spend any time with worldly people who live that way openly. They don't do the latter because of what it would do to their "testimony," and all while the whole Church conspires to wreck their collective testimony by means of culpable silence.

OH, WELL

> But now I have written unto you not to keep company, if any man that is called a brother be a fornicator, or covetous, or an idolater, or a railer, or a drunkard, or an extortioner; with such an one no not to eat. For what have I to do to judge them also that are without? do not ye judge them that are within? But them that are without God judgeth. Therefore put away from among yourselves that wicked person. (1 Cor. 5:11–13)

The key phrase here is "called a brother." This is not simply a matter of self-identification, because Paul then goes on to use the objective categories of "without" and "within." The person concerned is in some sense a member of the Christian community. So, if he is called a brother, and behaves in certain specified ways, then we are not to eat with such a person. The "not eat" in verse 11 here is tantamount to excommunication, to a formal putting away. The last injunction here is a quotation from multiple places in Deuteronomy (17:7; 19:19; 22:21, 24; 24:7), all of which refer to a formal process of expulsion from the covenant community.

Paul says that we do not have a duty to clean up the world—those who are "without." We have a duty to keep the sanctuary clean. As more and more of the world is brought into the Church, the behavior of these new converts becomes relevant. But until then, the Church is not to pursue worldlings in the name of Comstockery or wowserism.

What sorts of things should draw the disciplinary attention of the Church? Paul mentions six things here. The first is fornication, the second is greed, the third is idolatry, the forth is reviling, the fifth is drunkenness, and the last is swindling. In the modern Church at least two things on that list are more likely to get you nominated for the elder board than to result in you being brought up on charges. Oh, well.

CHAPTER 6

UNDERSTANDING THE REQUIREMENT

> Dare any of you, having a matter against another, go to law before the unjust, and not before the saints? (1 Cor. 6:1)

Before we delve into the reasons Paul gives for his standards about lawsuits, we need first to take a close look at what the standard actually is. The concern is this: members of the church at Corinth had a "matter" against a fellow member of the Church. They were taking their disputes before the unrighteous (*adikia*), or as he puts it in verse 6, unbelievers.

A lot of confusion has been caused by the quiet changing of this into a prohibition of Christians having something sorted out in *civil* court. If the civil court is run by unbelievers, and on unbelieving principles, then the Pauline prohibition of course applies. Christians should prefer to have their case adjudicated by the church janitor to airing their dirty laundry in front of unbelievers. But if the civil courts are Christian, and based on biblical law, as they have been at previous periods in our history, there would be no problem with having such cases heard there. That is where they would belong. This is foundational to understanding the argument that follows.

LAWSUITS AND POSTMILLENNIALISM

> Do ye not know that the saints shall judge the world? and if the world shall be judged by you, are ye unworthy to judge the smallest matters? Know ye not that we shall judge angels? how much more things that pertain to this life? (1 Cor. 6:2–3)

Before getting to his conclusion—that Christians should prefer being screwed by a fellow believer to being vindicated by an unbelieving judge against a fellow believer—the apostle Paul sets out the premises that he is reasoning from. Believers are the future judges of the world, and we do not practice for this role by having the world judge us. If we are destined to hear all their cases, then how is it preparation for them to hear all our cases?

The word judge here is not being used in the sense of the Last Judgment. The word is being used here as in the book of Judges—believers will be given rule over the world, and over the angels. God has made us kings and priests on the earth. The meek will inherit the earth, as somebody once said.

We are not yet in this condition of maturity, but like little children in the backyard playing at adult roles, we should be in training for this condition of maturity. One of the ways we train for this is by exercising mature wisdom within the Church over "the smallest matters." And if we are faithful in little, we will be given responsibility for much.

One of the reasons why many Christians have trouble with Paul's conclusions is that they really don't like his premises at all.

INFIDELITY, NOT REALISM

> If then ye have judgments of things pertaining to this life, set them to judge who are least esteemed in the church. (1 Cor. 6:4)

Paul says that before we should let unbelievers adjudicate our problems, we should rather have the responsibility for judging assigned to the least esteemed Christian in the church that we know. What is the worst thing that could happen? The worst thing that could happen would be for the case to be decided in the wrong way, and it goes against you—and when you were in the right. It would be better for that to happen, Paul argues, than for the gaudy spectacle of the whole case going against the gospel, the grace of God, the redemptive purposes of God for the world, and Christ crucified—and all in front of unbelievers.

And *gaudy spectacle* is the right word. I have seen Christian leaders who were more concerned for the dog in their particular fight than they were for the message God has given to a lost world. Paul's phrase from the next verse comes to mind—I speak this to your *shame*. Going to court in front of unbelievers is not realism; it is infidelity.

LAWSUITS AS ESCHATOLOGICAL FAILURE

> I speak to your shame. Is it so, that there is not a wise man among you? no, not one that shall be able to judge between his brethren? But brother goeth to law with brother, and that before the unbelievers. (1 Cor. 6:5–6)

The dispute between brothers is one level of failure, but it is the willingness to have that dispute adjudicated by unbelievers that really astonishes Paul. What? Why would a church want to publicly admit that they don't contain within their ranks a man wise enough to serve as a judge in cases like this?

The fact that former colleagues or business partners are now on opposite sides of an awful breech is one kind of failure, but it is part of living in a fallen world. But Paul has his eye on the new world that is forming in and through the Church. And when the Church lets this kind of thing go, they are saying (in effect) that the new world is failing also. But if the new world is to fail, then what is the whole point? Why are we doing this at all?

CUTTING THE BABY IN TWO

> Now therefore there is utterly a fault among you, because ye go to law one with another. Why do ye

not rather take wrong? why do ye not rather suffer yourselves to be defrauded? Nay, ye do wrong, and defraud, and that your brethren. (1 Cor. 6:7–8)

Paul has made it quite clear that brothers are not to haul their grievances into courts controlled by unbelievers. The behavior is appalling on many levels, and in this part of the passage Paul shows us just how important the principle is. He says that rather than ask unbelievers to sort through the dirty laundry of Christians, the Christians concerned should be willing to suffer loss instead. I should therefore prefer to lose my shirt to a fellow believer than to get that shirt back, courtesy of an unbelieving judge.

Just to be clear, this is not unclear. In addition, the principle doesn't change as the amounts get larger. One man might be willing to suffer loss if it is ten bucks, but if it a thousand bucks, he would argue his case before unbelievers, and would do so with the veins on his neck sticking out.

But we should be careful. Paul appears to have set a trap for us. In verse 7, he says that we should rather be defrauded financially by a fellow Christian than to have the name of Christ defrauded in our public testimony. But when a believer responds to the apostle by saying "that's not realistic," or "surely he doesn't expect me to just accept this loss," the apostle anticipates us with his response. No, he says, you do wrong, and you defraud. This means that the person unwilling to be defrauded is the one who is actually guilty, at some level, of fraud. Like Solomon, the apostle Paul offers to cut the baby in two.

SINS ARE LIKE GRAPES

> Know ye not that the unrighteous shall not inherit the kingdom of God? Be not deceived: neither fornicators, nor idolaters, nor adulterers, nor effeminate, Nor abusers of themselves with mankind, nor thieves, nor covetous, nor drunkards, nor revilers, nor extortioners, shall inherit the kingdom of God. And such were some of you: but ye are washed . . . (1 Cor. 6:9–11a)

There are three things to note about this passage. The first is to mark how naturally it follows from his previous assertions about Christians in lawsuits with one another. He has just finished telling us that the true path to take is that of being more willing to suffer fraud than to disgrace the gospel by arguing your case in front of unbelievers. But no, he says, "ye do wrong, and defraud." Refusal to be defrauded is actually an admission that you are hell-bent on defrauding someone else. Paul says this, and moves right into "Know ye not that the unrighteous shall not inherit ..." and he begins with a laundry list of big ticket sexual sins. So depend upon it—if a professing Christian is willing to get down and dirty in unbelieving courtrooms with fellow Christians, no one should be surprised two years later when the mistresses, or the porn, or the child abuse, or the sodomy come into view. Sins are like grapes; they come in bunches.

The second thing to note is that he says twice that a certain class of people will not inherit the kingdom of God. He emphasizes this because it is easy to miss—in fact he warns us not to be deceived on the point. Those who fornicate, those who worship idols, those who commit adultery, those who are catamites, those who are sodomites, those who steal, those who covet, those who get drunk, those who revile, those who extort are all lost and condemned. They will not inherit the kingdom. But there is no reason to lose hope. The ranks of the Corinthian church were filled up with people who had all those sins and more filling up their resume. There is not a sin on that list that can't cause someone to miss inheriting the kingdom, and there is not a sin on that list that can't be washed clean.

For those who like to pretend that the Scriptures are ambiguous about homosexual sin, the reverse is the case. The reference to catamites and sodomites is very specific—these are two kinds of male homosexuals, the kind the plays the passive, receptive role, and the one who plays the active, male role. But whether the man is pitching or catching, the sin is unrighteousness that shuts him out of the kingdom of God.

And third, it should be noted that these are all high-handed shameless sins—and it is not surprising that the apostle had to speak to them about their *shame* (v. 5). When you are not ashamed when you ought to be, it is often the case that you are not ashamed later when you *really* ought to be.

CALLED FROM WHERE?

> And such were some of you: but ye are washed, but ye are sanctified, but ye are justified in the name of the Lord Jesus, and by the Spirit of our God. (1 Cor. 6:11)

When Paul tells the Corinthians "and such were some of you," he is saying that God's company of saints is made up of what used to be the worst of the worst. They were all sanctified in Christ Jesus (1 Cor. 1:2), they were all called to be saints (1 Cor. 1:2). That is to say, they were called to be holy ones. According to this passage, where were they called *from*? When a mother calls her children in for dinner, she calls them in from the backyard. Where did God call His saints *from*? The answer is that He called them from fornication, idolatry, adultery, and sodomy (1 Cor. 6:9). He called them from thievery, covetousness, drunkenness, reviling, and extortion (1 Cor. 6:10).

In the name of Jesus (that is, by the authority of Jesus), three gifts were given to this rabble. The gifts were made effective by the Spirit of God—He is the one who brought the gifts to bear. The three gifts are washing, sanctification, and justification. In the name of Jesus, the Holy Spirit cleans us up, sets us apart, and declares us righteous.

UNLAWFUL TO HIT BOTTOM

> All things are lawful unto me, but all things are not expedient: all things are lawful for me, but I will not be brought under the power of any. (1 Cor. 6:12)

Paul has just finished telling us that adulterers and thieves and whatnot will not inherit the kingdom of God. So when he says here that "all things are lawful," he is clearly not referring to the sort of thing he has just finished talking about. It would be truly odd for an apostle to argue that going to Hell was lawful, just not expedient.

In the illustration that immediately follows ("meat for the belly," v. 13), it becomes clear that Paul is now talking about lawful things in themselves which have the capacity to bring a man under their authority in an unhelpful way. Adultery is always *malum in se*, evil in itself. Marriage is a lawful state; it is an ordinance of God. But sinful men often pursue it for the wrong reasons, or in the wrong way. The same goes for food and wine, more good gifts from the Lord. All foods are lawful, including processed corn, but not all foods are expedient. Paul here is concerned with being brought into bondage by something that is otherwise lawful.

If Paul is so careful about created gifts from God, for which we might come to have a disordered appetite, what would he say to a teenager who thinks smoking cigarettes is the coolest thing? He would say lawful . . . but certainly not expedient. And when the kid has been "brought under the power" of it, then it is no longer lawful. It was lawful to jump off the cliff, but it was unlawful to hit bottom. People who give their bodies extra dependencies to fight off are saying, in effect, that the normal course of Christian sanctification is way too easy for them. They want to undertake their earthly pilgrimage with one hand tied behind their back. They are *so* strong.

RESURRECTION TRANSFORMATION

> Meats for the belly, and the belly for meats: but God shall destroy both it and them. Now the body is not for fornication, but for the Lord; and the Lord for the body. And God hath both raised up the Lord, and will also raise up us by his own power. (1 Cor. 6:13–14)

In this passage, Paul is giving us a glimpse of our physical life on the other side of the resurrection. The kind of food we have now and the kind of belly we have now will both be destroyed. This ought not to be understood as a subtraction, as though all the food will be taken away in the Great Marriage Supper of the Lamb. No, our kind of food will be taken away, not because it is the real kind of food, but rather for the opposite reason. Our food in the here and now is pretty thin soup—not adequate for the realities of that greater banquet. For that reason, our idea of food and our kind of belly will be "destroyed."

Paul reasons analogously with the matter of fornication. The body is for the Lord, and the Lord is for the body. Something beyond all mortal reckoning is going to happen to us in the resurrection, concerning which transformation our experience with sex in this life is just a dim flicker. Marital love in this life prepares us for that time, while fornication is a disrupting or retarding influence. So if our bodies are "for the Lord," we ought not to do anything with our bodies now that interferes with God's plan.

If sex as we know it exists in Heaven, then the Sadducean question stands. "Whose wife will she be?" Sex as we know it would necessitate polygamy and polyandry in the resurrection. But it does not follow from this that God has exhausted all the options. God is good.

ONE SPIRIT, ONE FLESH

> Know ye not that your bodies are the members of Christ? shall I then take the members of Christ, and make them

> the members of an harlot? God forbid. What? know ye not that he which is joined to an harlot is one body? for two, saith he, shall be one flesh. But he that is joined unto the Lord is one spirit. (1 Cor. 6:15–17)

We are dealing here with two mysterious kinds of bodily union. There is the physical one-flesh union that occurs between a man and a woman in sexual intercourse, and there is another kind of union between mankind and Christ, of which the first kind of union is a type.

Someone who is joined to the Lord is "one spirit" with Him, but this spiritual union is not an ethereal union. We can see this within the teaching of this passage because a Christian's body is counted, on the basis of this spiritual union, as being a "member of Christ." Moreover, if a Christian man sleeps with a prostitute, he is taking the holiness of that membership into the bed with him. So if a man is united to Christ in "this way," and united to a prostitute "that way," then this means that the members of Christ are taken to the prostitute, and made members of her. The two kinds of union are therefore "relatable"—they have something to do with one another.

Sexual union within marriage gives us a pure typology, as Paul shows us in the fifth chapter of Ephesians. This is a great mystery, Paul says, but he is speaking of Christ and the Church. We will not have sex in the resurrection, but we will have something much more glorious: we will have the antitype. Sexual union apart from marriage gives us an impure typology. Among its other pollutions and faults, fornication is also false teaching.

HE CALLS THE SHOTS

> Flee fornication. Every sin that a man doeth is without the body; but he that committeth fornication sinneth against his own body. What? know ye not that your body is the temple of the Holy Ghost which is in you, which ye have of God, and ye are not your own? For ye are bought with a price: therefore glorify God in your body, and in your spirit, which are God's. (1 Cor. 6:18–20)

This passage contains one of the most abused verses in Scripture. What Paul says about fornication, and expressly limits to fornication *only*, has come by zealots to be applied to cigars, refined sugar, whiskey and wine, insufficient exercise, processed corn, and whatever the nemesis of the next great health fad might be.

All other sins, Paul says, assuming them to be sins, are not against the body in the sense that fornication is. And to sin against the body in *this* sense is sacrilege, because it brings un-covenanted union into the temple of all true covenants. Paul goes right to the heart of the issue. If our bodies are part of this temple, then we ought not to desecrate the temple. Further, if we are part of this temple of the Holy Spirit, this means that we do not belong to ourselves. We are not our own. The only way to be incorporated into the temple is to be purchased for that end. We were bought with a price.

Since we were purchased and are owned by another, we have no authorization to make sexually immoral decisions. My body does not belong to me—and so I am called to make decisions that glorify God in my body, and in my spirit. Both belong to God, and so He makes all the sexual decisions. He calls the shots.

CHAPTER 7

TOUCHING A WOMAN AND THE PRESENT DISTRESS

> Now concerning the things whereof ye wrote unto me: It is good for a man not to touch a woman. (1 Cor. 7:1)

The first thing to note is the phrase "concerning the things whereof ye wrote." Reading this epistle is like listening to one half of a phone conversation. The Corinthians had written a list of questions for Paul, and he was working his way through the answers. One of the things we have to do, therefore, if we are to understand this epistle correctly, is to reconstruct the questions rightly. The context of the question affects the intent and meaning of the answers.

If we treat Paul's statement here ("good for a man not to touch a woman") as an absolute that fell from the timeless sky, we will draw erroneous and unbiblical conclusions about marriage. Marriage will be thought of as somehow "less good" than the ideal state of affairs found in verse 1, where the man is urged to keep his hands in his pockets.

But a bit later in this chapter a bit more of the context of the question leaks out. Paul says there that "this is good *for the present* distress . . . it is good for a man so to be" (v. 26). It is one thing to be told that if you don't deny Christ you will be thrown to the lions. It is another to be told that if you don't deny Christ you, your wife, and three little children will be thrown to the lions. But this emergency situation was just a temporary one; the "time is short" (v. 29). Reasoning by analogy, we can conclude that the same counsel is good for comparable situations down throughout the history of the Church. But even then, even in times of impending persecution, the encumbrances and cares of marriage are to be preferred to trap of fornication (v. 2).

Compare this to our time, when the encumbrances of porn are preferred to the liberation of marriage. We should write the apostle Paul a *different* list of questions.

AN EARTHLY SOLUTION

> Nevertheless, to avoid fornication, let every man have his own wife, and let every woman have her own husband. Let the husband render unto the wife due

benevolence: and likewise also the wife unto the husband. (1 Cor. 7:2–3)

When Paul says that it is good for a man "not to touch a woman," he is talking about the time of "present distress" only. But even there, he is clear that while it would be tough to go through a time of persecution with a wife and kids (v. 33), it would be even tougher to go through such a time as a fornicator.

Paul knows that he has a peculiar gift, that of celibacy (v. 7). He also knows (and tells us) just how rare that gift is. In these verses, he assumes that "every" man should have his own wife. He assumes that "every" woman should have her own husband. If the occasional one-off gift of celibacy doesn't keep Paul from saying that everybody should be married, still less would the mythical and very modern "gift of singleness" keep him from saying it. Many men who celebrate the gift of singleness are actually celebrating the luxuries of irresponsibility. Mark Driscoll says, rightly, that men are like trucks. They drive straighter and smoother when they have a load.

Paul is saying that fornication is an important thing to avoid, so much so that a man should be willing to take on a great deal of responsibility rather than fall into such sin—and I am talking about an amount of responsibility that many today with the "gift of singleness" appear to be allergic to. Such responsibility is God's answer to computer porn. Both the husband and the wife are instructed to render themselves freely to the other, with the possible temptations of the other in mind. In a godly marriage, the existence of such temptations is not resented, but rather addressed in a very earthy and practical way. God's solution to sexual temptation is sex, and a goodly amount of it.

SEXUAL RECIPROCITY

> The wife hath not power of her own body, but the husband: and likewise also the husband hath not power of his own body, but the wife. (1 Cor. 7:4)

Here is another reason for recognizing that Paul did not give the advice found in verse 1 because he was sexually uptight or repressed in any way. He was concerned about the impending distress (v. 26), but was very realistic about the human frame. Sex is not really optional (v. 2).

Having urged marriage as a remedy for fornication, he now urges men and women to adopt the mindset that would make ongoing application of that remedy a possibility. What he teaches here is reciprocity of sexual authority. The wife does not own her own body, but the authority over it (*exousia*) belongs to her husband. This by itself would reduce marriage to a lower form of concubinage, but Paul does not stop there. The same authority that a man has over a woman sexually is an authority that she may wield over him. Sexual authority is reciprocal.

They can have this mutual authority in a workable way only because God has authority over the whole thing. For example, we learn (v. 5) that this authority has limits—a man and wife do not get to combine their authority and decided to separate sexually for extended periods of time—whether from misguided asceticism or mutual resentments. It doesn't matter. Married couples are called by God to act like married couples.

This does not mean that there should be "due benevolence" negotiations, like it was a business deal, but it does mean that there should be some conversations about it.

SEXUAL FRAUD

> Defraud ye not one the other, except it be with consent for a time, that ye may give yourselves to fasting and prayer; and come together again, that Satan tempt you not for your incontinency. But I speak this by permission, and not of commandment. (1 Cor. 7:5–6)

Paul requires an ongoing sexual relationship for married couples, assuming that it is an essential aspect of the married life. He allows one exception, and that exception would consist of a short sexual fast, agreed upon by mutual consent, and coupled with a season of prayer and fasting from food. Trying to go beyond this short period is to set yourselves up for sexual temptations from Satan. In this statement, Paul is allowing for short sexual fasts, and not requiring them.

It is striking that Paul describes sexual abstinence that do not meet these requirements as a species of fraud. When a husband or wife pulls away from their spouse sexually, outside of this kind of situation, that person is stealing. Bitterness, grievances, resentments, and so on, do not give a person grounds for fraud. If a man is bitter against his neighbor, this does not provide grounds for sneaking over in the middle of the night and taking his stuff, or running a fraudulent scam operation against him. In the same way, and for the same reasons, husbands and wives do not have the right to go on strike. If grievous sin has made sexual relations impossible—as does happen—then it is time for divorce.

CELIBACY AND SINGLENESS

> For I would that all men were even as I myself. But every man hath his proper gift of God, one after this manner, and another after that. I say therefore to the unmarried and widows, It is good for them if they abide even as I. But if they cannot contain, let them marry: for it is better to marry than to burn. (1 Cor. 7:7–9)

As is the nature with all individuals, Paul thinks in terms of his own giftedness. He wishes that all men had his gift; he is a contented man, and he sees the blessing in what has been bestowed on him. He doesn't have the burdens and responsibilities of married life, and he doesn't have the distractions of sexual temptation. Paul's gift here is a rare one, and it is the gift of celibacy. This is quite distinct from the mythical gift of "singleness" that many young men today think they have. If it needs to be supported by porn, it isn't the gift of celibacy.

At the same time, Paul is good about not being imperialistic with his own gifts. He enjoys it, and wishes other men could enjoy it too, but he knows that God is the one who apportions all gifts. He has given a handful of individuals the gift of celibacy. So if someone happens to find himself in a single state—unmarried or widowed—Paul's advice is to remain in that state (again, in the light of the impending distress mentioned in v. 26). Nevertheless, present distress or not, impending persecution or not, if a person cannot contain himself sexually, then they need to marry. As Paul puts it, famously, it is better to marry than to burn. It would be better to go into a persecution with the responsibilities of a wife and family than to go into a persecution with a pattern of fornication on your conscience.

NOT I, BUT THE LORD

> And unto the married I command, yet not I, but the Lord, Let not the wife depart from her husband (1 Cor. 7:10)

In order to understand Paul rightly here, we have to grasp what he means by "not I, but the Lord." This is too often assumed to be Paul exempting his instructions in this matter from any claim of authoritative inspiration. In other words, this is taken as Paul just giving his personal opinion in verse 12, as opposed to the inspired requirement he lays down in verse 10. I believe we have to reject this, and take the argument in another direction entirely.

The marriage tangles that arose in Corinth could be divided into two broad categories. The first was the kind of situation in a Gentile church like Corinth that had a parallel in the covenant of Israel—what is our view of divorce when it concerns two believers, two covenant members? The Lord, during the course of His earthly ministry, taught on this directly. Paul is simply applying the marriage teaching from the Gospels to the situation at Corinth. This teaching did not originate with him, Paul says, and he says this by saying "not I, but the Lord."

But when he gets to verse 12, he is addressing a circumstance that would have been common in the new churches among the Gentiles, and comparatively rare among the Jews in Israel. What do we do with questions about divorce when it is a mixed marriage? One spouse was converted, and the other was not. Now what? This would have been a regular problem in a place like Corinth, and the Lord's teaching in the Gospels did not address it. It was therefore a circumstance that called for apostolic legislation.

If we keep this distinction clear in our minds, it will help us a great deal as we work through the remainder of this section.

A BAD CHRISTIAN MARRIAGE

> And unto the married I command, yet not I, but the Lord, Let not the wife depart from her husband: But and if she depart, let her remain unmarried, or be reconciled to her husband: and let not the husband put away his wife. (1 Cor. 7:10–11)

Recall that this is Paul's summary and application of the Lord's teaching on marriage, as it applies to two members of the covenant. In the new covenant, this means that these two verses are addressing a troubled marriage of two professing Christians. It is clear from what Paul says here that the exception clause that the Lord gives (except for *porneias*) is not yet operative, which means that we have two Christians who cannot get along. This is therefore not a situation where the marriage vow has been broken through some form of infidelity, but rather what the Lord described as Moses making allowance for the problem of hard hearts.

In such circumstances, Paul says, a wife should not leave her husband. We can see the Lord's restrictions coming into play next, because Paul then says that if the situation is bad enough that the wife has to leave, she should make a point to remain unmarried. This fits perfectly with what the Lord taught—if she leaves, but there has been no *porneias*, and she then she marries another, then that is tantamount to adultery. So, if she has to separate, which is sometimes necessary, don't compound the problems by marrying another.

One other thing is important to note. If she has to separate (for the sake of her safety, say), and her husband is a professing Christian whose behavior has been horrendous, one of the things that should happen is that the Church should discipline him. If he is unrepentant, and chases his wife away, and the Church excommunicates him, then he is judicially an unbeliever, and then Paul's instructions about mixed marriage (v. 12ff) would then apply.

PLEASED TO BE TOGETHER

> But to the rest speak I, not the Lord: If any brother hath a wife that believeth not, and she be pleased to dwell with him, let him not put her away. And the woman which hath an husband that believeth not, and if he be pleased to dwell with her, let her not leave him. (1 Cor. 7:12–13)

Paul then moves into uncharted territory. The Lord's teaching on divorce presupposed two members of the covenant.

But because of the expansion of the gospel into the pagan world, a new situation had arisen—that of mixed marriages. Now what? So Paul is not saying that this teaching is uninspired, while the earlier standard was inspired by the Lord. The earlier teaching came from the Lord Jesus in His earthly ministry, and this teaching came from Paul's apostolic ministry.

So what was that teaching? The bottom line is that mere unbelief on the part of a spouse is *not* grounds for divorce. This means having sex with a pagan is not automatically contaminating for the believer.

The word that is used in both verses, applied to both sexes, is *suneudokeo*—pleased to be together with. This presupposes a willingness on the part of the unbeliever to live within the confines of a biblical definition of marriage. If he or she is willing for that, then the marriage should continue. If the situation is one of animus and open hostility, then the circumstances don't fit with Paul's hypothetical situation. But even there, Paul assumes that it will be the unbeliever who departs (v. 15). The believer may have to take the initiative at some point, especially if the unbeliever is adept at passive aggressive games, but if at all possible the hostility of desertion should be the work of the hostile one.

If a Christian is the hostile one, and departs from a fellow Christian without biblical warrant, and there has been no *porneias*, then that Christian should be disciplined by the Church for his or her actions. Once that has happened, their judicial status is that of an unbeliever, and the teaching of this passage applies.

CHILDREN AS SAINTS

> For the unbelieving husband is sanctified by the wife, and the unbelieving wife is sanctified by the husband: else were your children unclean; but now are they holy. (1 Cor. 7:14)

The Corinthians had wanted to know whether unbelief on the part of a spouse was in itself grounds for divorce. Paul has replied no, provided that the unbelieving partner is pleased to be together with the Christian in a marriage as biblically defined. If the only thing that is wrong is the spouse's failure to believe in Christ, then the couple should still remain together.

But isn't it somehow a spiritual contaminant to have sex with a pagan? No, Paul argues. A Christian ought not to *marry* a non-Christian (2 Cor. 6:14), but once married to one, a Christian needs to be faithful to his vows regardless. That means being faithful to all the vows, including the sexual commitment. But sex is an activity that often results in children. What about the children? Won't the offspring of a mixed marriage be outside the covenant? No, Paul replies again. In this regard, the new covenant is not like the old. In the old covenant, the unclean contaminated the clean (Haggai 2:13–14). Jesus reversed this order—He would make the unclean clean by coming in contact with it (Mark 5:25).

And this means that in a mixed marriage, when the wife conceives a child, that child is not unclean, but rather holy. The word for *holy* here is *hagia*—and this is striking because when this word is applied to persons, it is almost always translated or rendered as *saints*. A child of at least one believing parent is a saint, and is to be treated as such.

NOT STACKING BRICKS

> But if the unbelieving depart, let him depart. A brother or a sister is not under bondage in such cases: but God hath called us to peace. For what knowest thou, O wife, whether thou shalt save thy husband? or how knowest thou, O man, whether thou shalt save thy wife? (1 Cor. 7:15–16)

One of the reasons why a believing spouse might hang on too long in an unworkable marriage is through a false assumption that time has the power to convert people. But Paul challenges this. How do you know (wife or husband) that continuation in ongoing marital strife is going to result in salvation for them? We know that we are dealing with strife because Paul reminds the believer here that we are called to peace, even if that peace means letting the source of the conflict go. Refusing to let someone go who is insistent on going their own way is a way of disrupting the peace—which may be more of a barrier to conversion than a divorce would be.

"Not under bondage" means not under bondage. If an unbelieving spouse is not "pleased to be together with" and departs, Paul says not to fight it. For some Christians to add, as many unfortunately do, that the deserted spouse is prohibited from remarriage later on is to say—and not too obliquely—that they are too under bondage.

This places a good deal of weight on what is meant by "pleased to be together with." It obviously doesn't mean a shared commitment to the central issues of life (for that would make them both believers), and at the other end of the spectrum it doesn't mean ten screaming fits a day. The way I would describe it is a willingness on the part of both husband and wife to function together as civilized human beings in a marriage relationship, sexual relations included.

Obviously, complications can arise easily. What about someone who is clearly not converted, but who is a baptized covenant member? Now what? If they are in the church of a pastor who is asking the question, he is in a position to resolve that. If a disobedient church member is not "pleased to be together with" the obedient one, and deserts, he should be disciplined for it. Once he is disciplined, he is judicially a non-believer, and this passage applies.

But in the messiness of this poor old world, the situations are not always that clean. The disobedient spouse did his thing at their previous church, which didn't do anything about it, and now the wronged spouse has moved to your town, joined your church, and has asked what her status is. A wise pastor should always remember he is pastoring sheep, not stacking bricks, and he should take care to reason—*mutatis mutandis*—in a way that protects the innocent, not the guilty. Often you can tell which party is the innocent one—the one who is more willing to put up with the lunkheadedness of our legalisms.

One last thing—we live in a time when divorce is far too easy to come by. The fact that these things can happen doesn't mean that they should. Divorce really does do a lot of damage to the kids, and mixed couples who can do it should labor to stay together for the sake of the kids, just as they labor to feed and clothe them. From either perspective it should be worth it.

TAKE IT FROM THERE

> But as God hath distributed to every man, as the Lord hath called every one, so let him walk. And so ordain I in all churches. (1 Cor. 7:17)

Paul concludes his passage on mixed marriage and divorce with his statement of a particular principle, one that serves as an introduction of his next point, which is in another area of life. That next point concerns the differences that existed between Jew and Gentile, between circumcised and uncircumcised. The principle is that every Christian should remember that God takes us from where we are, and not from where we should have been.

God is in the process of redeeming a fallen world, restoring it, which is not the same thing as arranging do-overs. When Paul says "so let him walk," he is saying that each one should walk from where he is. Tying this in with what went before, where were you when the Lord first called you? Halfway through the divorce already? A single mom? Married to an atheist college professor? What Paul ordained in all the churches is that we should take it from there.

WHEN THE SPIRIT BREAKS THE RULES

> Is any man called being circumcised? let him not become uncircumcised. Is any called in uncircumcision?

let him not be circumcised. Circumcision is nothing, and uncircumcision is nothing, but the keeping of the commandments of God. (1 Cor. 7:18–19)

Paul's principle is that every man should begin to walk with God from the place where God called him. This principle applies to difficult marriages to pagans, and it applies to marriages that have fallen apart because of it. The principle is now applied to the cultural and religious categories of Jew and Gentile, circumcised and uncircumcised (vv. 18–19). In a moment he is going to apply the principle to those who were called to Christ while in the condition of slavery (v. 21ff).

Again, keeping the commandment of God is what counts—and this means that we are to do what God requires and in the way He requires it. Our circumstances change, but God does not change. Because we serve an unchanging God in the midst of changing circumstances, that means that we must not be wooden in our obedience. We have a constant tendency to want to freeze what obedience looks like, and we want to do this because we don't want to think with our minds or with our hearts. But such a refusal is not maturity, and we are called to maturity.

This is why God can tell His saints to build His Temple, and God can then tear it down with heathen armies. This is why He can command sacrifices, and then inspire the psalmist to say that sacrifices "You did not require." This is why He can tell us to be merciful and to offer sacrifices, and then tell us that He desires mercy and not sacrifice. This is why Paul can say here that circumcision, given to

Abraham as a glorious thing, is nothing. This is why he can say that uncircumcision is nothing. As in, God does not care.

And we are good with this, because the text is talking about other people's precious things. But how about this? Baptism is nothing, and lack of baptism is nothing. Liturgy is nothing. The church calendar is nothing. Glorious music in worship is nothing. But . . . but . . . we are doing these things in obedience, and keeping God's commandments is what counts. Well, then, great. Keep after it. That is the work of faith, and God never fights the work of His own Spirit.

Just remember that His own Spirit will often contradict what we all thought He told us to do. That is where reformations come from.

AS YOU WERE WHEN CALLED

> Let every man abide in the same calling wherein he was called. Art thou called being a servant? care not for it: but if thou mayest be made free, use it rather. For he that is called in the Lord, being a servant, is the Lord's freeman: likewise also he that is called, being free, is Christ's servant. Ye are bought with a price; be not ye the servants of men. Brethren, let every man, wherein he is called, therein abide with God. (1 Cor. 7:20–24)

Paul acknowledges that God is the one who writes every story; He is the one who directs each of our lives. This means that we must assume that He knew the position we would be in at the time He called us to Himself. We do not resign ourselves to that condition forever and ever, with a kind of fatalism, but neither are we to panic as though something terrible has happened.

The example of this principle Paul turns to now involves slavery—a condition of servitude. Paul says that if a man was called to Christ while a slave, he ought not to be anxious over the fact. Remain there, Paul teaches. But if a natural opportunity for freedom comes, then take it. Freedom is better than slavery, but agitation over slavery while a slave just makes the slavery worse. Paul here prohibits Christians from becoming slaves voluntarily, and he urges slaves to become free as they have opportunity. But the way a person comes to freedom is very important . . . otherwise, he will just bring his slavery with him, and it will turn into a different kind of slavery. A number of the slaves that Moses liberated remained in slavery in the wilderness.

A slave should therefore live as Christ's freeman—and if he is set free, he will be ready. And a man who is free should live as Christ's slave, which in turn will prepare him for any eventuality. A man should assume that God wants him to be in the condition he was in when he was converted, unless providentially led to another condition.

THE PRINCIPLE AND THE OCCASION

> Now concerning virgins I have no commandment of the Lord: yet I give my judgment, as one that hath obtained mercy of the Lord to be faithful. I suppose therefore that this is good for the present distress, I say, that it is good for a man so to be. (1 Cor. 7:25–26)

The principle is that every Christian should start with contentment in the place where he was when God called him. This principle applies to those who are married, to those who are married to an amiable unbeliever, to those who are married to a hostile unbeliever, to those who are unmarried but in control of their lusts, to those who are unmarried and not in control of them, to those who are circumcised, to those who are uncircumcised, to those who are slaves, and to those who are not.

The occasion in which Paul is applying this principle is the time of the "present distress" (v. 26). It is one thing to stand up for Christ under the threat of being thrown to the lions; it is another thing to stand up for Him under threat of your small children being thrown to the lions. Because of the impending persecution, Paul says that this is not a good time (everything else being equal) to start a family. At the same time, a man who is consumed by his lusts will fare even worse during a time of persecution, and so Paul gives some folks permission to get married, present distress and all.

In these verses, he returns to the unmarried who can contain themselves. Those virgins who can do so would be best advised to remain unmarried.

PAUL ON DIVORCE AND REMARRIAGE

> Art thou bound unto a wife? seek not to be loosed. Art thou loosed from a wife? seek not a wife. But and if thou marry, thou hast not sinned; and if a virgin marry, she hath not sinned. Nevertheless such shall have trouble in the flesh: but I spare you. (1 Cor. 7:27–28)

We now get into some of Paul's applications that have the capacity to cause consternation among the pious, and so we must proceed carefully. We have to remember that our responsibility is that of being biblical, which is not necessarily the same thing as being "strict."

Remember again the context of these exhortations, which is very much present in these recommendations. That context is the "present distress," mentioned in the previous verse. Because of the impending persecution, Christians need to make a point of traveling light if they can do so without falling into immorality.

That said, Paul says that the present distress is *not* grounds for seeking a divorce. Someone who is already bound in marriage should not seek to get free of his obligations (v. 27). But, in line with the previous instructions, someone who is already divorced should not seek a wife (v. 27). Again, this particular restriction on the divorced man is not because he is divorced and has cooties, but rather because of the present distress. Nevertheless, Paul goes on, if that same divorced man (that he is talking about) goes ahead and gets married, he has not sinned (v. 28). The same thing goes for a virgin, marrying for the first time (v. 28). Both the divorced man who marries again and the virgin who marries are going to have certain hardships in the flesh (again, because of the present distress), and Paul would like to spare them this.

It should go without saying that Paul is not here giving license to a divorced man whose remarriage would run contrary to the standards set out by the Lord Jesus (Matt. 19:8–9). But this Pauline instruction here does exclude an absolutist prohibition of remarriage under all possible circumstances.

NOT A MARRYING TIME

> But this I say, brethren, the time is short: it remaineth, that both they that have wives be as though they had none; And they that weep, as though they wept not; and they that rejoice, as though they rejoiced not; and they that buy, as though they possessed not; And they that use this world, as not abusing it: for the fashion of this world passeth away. (1 Cor. 7:29–31)

We have referred many times to the "present distress," which was the time of tribulation and persecution that Paul was anticipating. And as a time of tribulation, it had much in common with other periods of distress and persecution throughout the history of the world—and there are lessons here for the saints down through the history of the Church. The attitude of Job, acknowledging that the Lord gives and the Lord removes, is an attitude that should be owned and internalized by every believer. Blessed be the name of the Lord. We are called to travel lightly. All that we have, no matter who or where we are, should be surrendered before God, lifted up on an open palm. The Lord can place things there, and take them away. If we clench them in our fists, it is no additional trouble for God to take them away, but our fingers get broken.

But this moment that Paul is anticipating was also unique. He says that a time of trouble was coming, in which marital status would be irrelevant, weeping would be beside the point, rejoicing would be a morning mist, and purchasing things would add nothing to the real inventory. The believers in the first century were living in the transition of ages, and they were told to "use the world" in a way that did not abuse it. Paul gives as his reason for these marching orders the fact that "the form, shape, template, pattern" (*schema*) of this world was passing away. The very structure of the old Judaic aeon was about to go defunct. The Christian aeon was beginning, and the convulsions that would occur would make it not a marrying time.

EARTHLY, NOT WORLDLY

> But I would have you without carefulness. He that is unmarried careth for the things that belong to the Lord, how he may please the Lord: But he that is married careth for the things that are of the world, how he may please his wife. There is a difference also between a wife and a virgin. The unmarried woman careth for the things of the Lord, that she may be holy both in body and in spirit: but she that is married careth for the things of the world, how she may please her husband. And this I speak for your own profit; not that I may cast a snare upon you, but for that which is comely, and that ye may attend upon the Lord without distraction. (1 Cor. 7:32–35)

We have already pointed out that Paul believed the unmarried state created the possibility of "traveling light" during times of persecution, which Paul knew were on the way. He recommends that state, because of these circumstances, if it is possible. At the same time, Paul is realistic. A person without giftedness in celibacy, who falls periodically into immorality, would be better off with a wife and family during the persecution than with his browser history of porn sites in a time of persecution. Get married rather than sin, Paul teaches. But if you are truly able to stay clean, traveling light during that time of history was the way to go.

He explains this from both the vantage of the man and the woman. An unmarried man can focus on spiritual things entirely, the things of the Lord (v. 32). This shows that Paul is talking about someone dedicated to celibacy for spiritual reasons, not someone addicted to singleness, for selfish reasons. The married man has earthly responsibilities (which Paul elsewhere requires him to pick up), and those responsibilities involve pleasing his wife. He says this is "of the world," not in the sense of "worldly," but rather in the sense of earthly. The same thing is true of the married woman. She cares for the things "of the world" too, how she might please her husband (v. 34). Her responsibilities are earthly, not worldly.

He says that the unmarried virgin is holy (set apart) in both body and spirit, in a way that enables her to care for the things of the Lord. Married believers are also holy, also consecrated, but the dedication is routed differently. Virginity is not exalted as a timeless principle of worth, but there are times when it makes perfect sense. Paul is not trying to trip anybody up (v. 35), but rather wants to profit them in a tough time.

PARTNERS IN CELIBACY

> But if any man think that he behaveth himself uncomely toward his virgin, if she pass the flower of her age, and need so require, let him do what he will, he sinneth not:

let them marry. Nevertheless he that standeth stedfast in his heart, having no necessity, but hath power over his own will, and hath so decreed in his heart that he will keep his virgin, doeth well. So then he that giveth her in marriage doeth well; but he that giveth her not in marriage doeth better. (1 Cor. 7:36–38)

The two ways this passage is usually taken are, in my mind, highly problematic. In one instance, the man is the young girl's father, but the language Paul uses here has to do with that same man's ability to control himself. This makes the situation at worst incestuous, and at best kind of creepy. Clearly, given Paul's understanding of biblical law, and the fact that he is an inspired apostle, that option should be excluded. The other interpretation is that the man he is talking about is the girl's betrothed. But this collides with our unwillingness to actually put Paul's advice into practice—when there is pending distress, stay engaged without marrying as long as possible? Why be engaged at all? And to attribute the whole mess to a Pauline pronoun confusion creates problems for our doctrine of inspiration.

My take is that it would be better to look for a solution in certain first century practices that we have no experience with. That is what I think is happening here. We will work through the verses in subsequent installments, but a little background is necessary first.

It is a fact that the early Church experimented with a form of celibate marriage, and the experiments began pretty early. The *subintroductae* were celibate wives who lived with clerics, and a Greek name *agapetae* was applied to women who lived with laymen under a strict vow of celibacy. Cyprian discourages the whole thing, and the practice was finally condemned at the Councils of Elvira (305 A.D.) and Nicea (325 A.D.). I would argue along the lines of good riddance, but Charles Williams was more defensive of the idea, and called these condemnations one of the first triumphs of the "weaker brethren." He calls them the "innocent sheep who by mere volume of imbecility have trampled over many delicate and attractive flowers in Christendom." I would actually put Paul in the neighborhood of Cyprian—he provides a standing escape clause in the vows. If this practice is what Paul is regulating (and cautioning against), the passage makes a good deal more sense.

THAT CELIBATEY FEEL

> But if any man think that he behaveth himself uncomely toward his virgin, if she pass the flower of her age, and need so require, let him do what he will, he sinneth not: let them marry. (1 Cor. 7:36)

There are two aspects to a man's improper treatment of such a virgin. The first is obvious—if the couple is under a vow of celibacy, but his longing glances have less and less of that celibatey feel about them, more bedroom eyes than prayers in the cloister eyes, he should just knock it off and marry her. And the second way a man would treat his virgin in an unseemly way would be by ignoring what we would call her biological clock. Paul expressly mentions her age, and appears to be thinking about her desire for children. Under such circumstances, it is no sin to marry.

THREE ODDITIES

> Nevertheless he that standeth stedfast in his heart, having no necessity, but hath power over his own will, and hath so decreed in his heart that he will keep his virgin, doeth well. (1 Cor. 7:37)

This is where we see the true oddity of what Paul is describing here. If the man being described here is the young woman's *father*, then why does Paul speak of such things as "necessity," and "will power," and "decreeing in the heart." But if it is the young lady's *fiancé*, then why on earth would anyone, much less an apostle, encourage him to see how long he can go in a state of betrothed virginity? Now admittedly, the alternative that I am proposing here (that Paul is talking about celibate marriages) is every bit as odd as these two options, but it has the advantage of not being creepy—because both partners in the arrangement would have been part of the decision.

CONTEXTUAL ODDITY

> So then he that giveth her in marriage doeth well; but he that giveth her not in marriage doeth better. (1 Cor. 7:38)

A problem for this reading I propose is the translation "giveth" here. Unfortunately, the word used doesn't help us out much. The KJV renders *gamidzo* as "give in marriage," while the ESV takes *gamidzo* as meaning "marry." This appears to be a situation where context has to help us decide, and I am simply suggesting that the original context may be odder than we had supposed.

AT LIBERTY

> The wife is bound by the law as long as her husband liveth; but if her husband be dead, she is at liberty to be married to whom she will; only in the Lord. But she is happier if she so abide, after my judgment: and I think also that I have the Spirit of God. (1 Cor. 7:39–40)

The pending distress, which affected Paul's advice on whether to get married in the first place was a distress that was still pending if a married woman, for example, lost her husband by death. What then?

As long as he is alive, that consideration outranks all the others. If he has died, then Paul allows that she who is at liberty to marry again. He says in the next verse that his advice to all unmarried people would still apply here—and this advice is Spirit-led. Traveling light through persecution was a God-given strategy. But even here, he leaves the decision up to her. At liberty means at liberty.

Two other things should be noted. A widow gets to make her own decisions in this regard. She is now the head of that household, and Paul says she can marry "whom *she* will." The decision is up to her, and does not have to revert to father, or brothers, or anything like that. The second thing is the one restriction that Paul places on her—she must marry "in the Lord," she must marry a fellow Christian. An unequal yoke is a bad idea at all times, but it is particularly bad when it comes to marriage.

CHAPTER 8

AN EPIC COMB-OVER

> Now as touching things offered unto idols, we know that we all have knowledge. Knowledge puffeth up, but charity edifieth. And if any man think that he knoweth any thing, he knoweth nothing yet as he ought to know. (1 Cor. 8:1–2)

Paul then moves to the next topic, which had to do with eating things that had been offered up in idol worship. This was a real problem in a place like Corinth, where the meat available in the meat market had been offered up, just a short time before, on the altar of some demon or other. Is it lawful for Christians to eat something like that? And, of course, the answer is *yes* and *no*.

This is not a contradiction—it is lawful to eat such meat, unless by eating it you were also devouring your brother. Under such circumstances, you should refrain—not because of the meat, but rather because of your brother. Eating such meat is fine; eating your brother is not fine.

In an earlier situation, the Greeks had been asked to refrain from eating such meat for the sake of table fellowship with Jews (for whom such meat had been forbidden, but also had become repulsive to them). That had been the decision of the Jerusalem council (Acts 15:29). In this situation, the strong former pagan was asked to refrain (if necessary) for the sake of the weak former pagan. The weakness was this: If a brother who could not disassociate the meat from the idol worship saw a stronger Christian partaking (who *could* disassociate the two) and imitated him, he would obviously fall back into his former sin of idolatry. Modern examples would be a former pagan who could not yet disassociate drinking and drunkenness or rock music and getting stoned. The law of love is clear—don't sacrifice your brother on the altar of your liberty.

And so this is how Paul opens up this subject. Everybody has knowledge. Big whoop. Christianity 101 teaches us that an idol is nothing (v. 4). Paul is saying that an idol is nothing, and knowledge that an idol is nothing is *also* nothing. Idols are a vanity, and super-duper knowledge about the vanity of idols is also vanity. In other words, when knowledge is made into an idol, it doesn't fare any better than the other idols do. Knowledge, taken the wrong way, is not meat offered *to* an idol, it *is* a meat idol. Knowledge, taken that way, is just meatware.

LOVE AND EPISTEMOLOGY

> But if any man love God, the same is known of him.
> (1 Cor. 8:3)

This short statement is a hinge in this argument. Paul has just said that love builds up, and knowledge (of a certain kind) puffs up. If a man is puffed up by his knowledge, then his knowledge is not true knowledge—he does not yet know as he ought to know. But if he loves, then he does know as he ought to know.

In short, if he loves God, then he is known by God, which means (in turn) that he knows as he ought to know. This knowledge on the part of God is clearly not saying that when one of us starts loving God, then at that point, God's omniscience swims into focus. "Oh, *there* you are!" This is the knowledge of relationship, and not the knowledge of raw cognition. To say here that God knows a man is to say that the man in question loves God, and knows how to use his doctrinal knowledge in ways that are a blessing to fellow Christians. His doctrine is edifying.

It is important therefore to note that epistemology is linked to love. We can't know as we ought unless we are known by God, and we can't be known by God unless we love Him. Loving God is therefore the beginning of knowledge (Prov. 1:7; 9:10).

NOTHING IN THE WORLD

> As concerning therefore the eating of those things that are offered in sacrifice unto idols, we know that an

> idol is nothing in the world, and that there is none other God but one. (1 Cor. 8:4)

Here we learn that every form of false religion is superstitious at some level—that is, it makes something out of nothing. Compared to the true and living God, an idol is nothing in the world, and there is no God beside the Most High. It is important to note that Paul says that the idol is nothing in the world. He does not say that God is the Most High in Heaven, but that idols can be something on earth. When it comes to eating meat that has been sacrificed to an idol, there is no reason for abstaining from it that can be found in the meat itself. To attribute that kind of power to pagan worship is superstitious—even if the superstition is held by someone outside that pagan religion.

The meat is not demon-possessed. The earth is the Lord's and the fullness of it. Everything else being equal, it would be perfectly fine to have a BLT made from bacon that came from a pig that was slaughtered on the altar of Satan. This kind of freedom that Christ brings does not give power to Satan, but rather takes all his power away—because his power rests on the platform of deceptive superstition.

Years ago someone phoned my wife very concerned about a rumor she had heard about Proctor & Gamble being given over to Satan—it had something do with their logo of the crescent moon and stars, etc. Supposedly, one of their execs had said on television that their profits went straight to the Bad Place. My response was that if Satan had indeed gone in for soap manufacturing we Christians ought to consider this to be, on the whole, a net plus.

If it is a lie, then Christians ought to be the first to laugh at it. And every idol is a lie. Every idol pretending to be something in the world is actually nothing in the world.

UNCLEAN VERSUS IMAGINARY

> For though there be that are called gods, whether in heaven or in earth, (as there be gods many, and lords many,) But to us there is but one God, the Father, of whom are all things, and we in him; and one Lord Jesus Christ, by whom are all things, and we by him. (1 Cor. 8:5–6)

This is a place where our use of upper and lower case letters is quite helpful. There is one God, Maker of Heaven and earth, but there are many gods. These gods are among those things which are made (John 1:3), and so they are on the same side of the Creator/creature divide that we are. There is one Lord, but many lords. This can be said in the same spirit that confesses one King, but many kings. This is how Jesus Christ can be Lord of lords and King of kings (Rev. 17:14; 19:16).

So these gods and lords exist, but they exist in the realm of the creature—archangels, men, roly-poly bugs, and gods are all created beings. What the pagans called gods, the Bible calls demons (1 Cor. 10:20–21). An atheist doesn't believe that Apollo existed at all—Christians don't believe that he was what he claimed to be. Fallen angels were worshiped under false pretenses, but that is not the same thing as not being there at all. If Smith or Murphy persuaded men to bow down to them and worship them, that would be a bad sin. But it does not mean that Smith and Murphy don't exist.

The early father Lactantius spends a great deal of time showing how many of the pagan gods were originally human kings (largely from Crete). In a similar way, we can see how some of the gods were spiritual beings (not divine beings). The woman who could tell fortunes at Philippi had (as the text puts it in the original) the "spirit of a python" (Acts 16:16). She was a devotee of the god (or demon) Apollo. The high priestess of that cult was the Pythoness, dedicated to service at the place where Apollo had reputedly killed a great python. According to Scripture, she really could tell fortunes, and she really did have a demon. Her spirit was unclean, not imaginary.

In this place, it is confessed that there is one God, and we are "in Him." It is also confessed that there is one Lord, the Lord Jesus, and we are "by Him." Jesus was the one through whom everything was created, and so we are here by His power. We are in God and we are by the Son. It is this form of triune monotheism that drives out all uncleanness.

STUMBLING A WEAKER BROTHER

> Howbeit there is not in every man that knowledge: for some with conscience of the idol unto this hour eat it as a thing offered unto an idol; and their conscience being weak is defiled. (1 Cor. 8:7)

Paul here defines what is happening when a weaker brother is stumbled. There are two things in the world—one belongs to God (meat) and the other to the devil (false worship). Through the practice of idolatry those two things are tied together, and are deeply connected in the minds and hearts of those in bondage to the devil. When such a person is converted, he comes out of his idolatry, but is not yet free of that association.

A strong Christian, for whom there is no idolatrous connection between the meat and the idol it was offered to, eats the meat, and all that happens is that he has a good meal. Afterwards he sighs in gratitude and reflects on how the earth is the Lord's and the fullness thereof. But a weaker Christian, freshly converted from idolatry, sees the strong Christian doing this and says to himself that it must be alright to eat the meat (which it actually is), but *he* cannot do it without getting entangled in the idolatry again.

An analogous situation in our day would be an innocent thing (wine) associated with a sinful thing (a life of drunkenness). Someone converted out of drunkenness may have real trouble disassociating the two. What happens when he sees a strong Christian exercising his liberty with alcohol? Or take someone who had never listened to rock music without getting stoned first. What happens when he sees a stronger Christian listening to rock? He thinks he can do it . . . but he can't.

DEMON-POSSESSED MEAT

> But meat commendeth us not to God: for neither, if we eat, are we the better; neither, if we eat not, are we the worse. But take heed lest by any means this liberty of yours become a stumblingblock to them that are weak. (1 Cor. 8:8–9)

In short, no matter where the meat has been, the meat is not demon-possessed. The meat, considered in itself, is a *max nix* kind of thing. If we eat, we are not thereby improved. If we refrain, we are not thereby kept pure. So the issue is not to be found anywhere in the meat.

The issue is always a matter of relationships. You are eating in community. If you eat this kind of meat in the wrong community, then you are partaking of the table of demons (1 Cor. 10:21). If you eat this meat in the right community, but in the wrong way, you are not partaking of *koinonia* love. You are stumbling your brother.

The man who understands the meat issue is the stronger brother. The man who misunderstands the meat is the weaker brother. But the man who understands his brother is the loving brother. The man who understands that the importance of a brother is greater than the weakness of a brother is the loving brother.

NEVER MIND THE GARLIC BUTTER

> For if any man see thee which hast knowledge sit at meat in the idol's temple, shall not the conscience of him which is weak be emboldened to eat those things which are offered to idols; And through thy knowledge shall the weaker brother perish, for whom Christ died? (1 Cor. 8:10–11)

So here is the scenario. We have a man with a strong conscience and robust immune system, and he knows that idolatry is a bunch of nothing. He has knowledge, and so he goes to the restaurant attached to the idol-temple, and there has his sirloin. Best one he ever had, and the idolatry is far from his mind. All he is thinking about is the tenderness of the cut, and the garlic butter on the potatoes.

But a weaker brother sees him there. This weaker brother is defined as someone who cannot (because of his personal history) disassociate the meat from the false worship. This being the case, if he eats the meats, he is sucked back into the idolatry. The stronger brother can swim in that current, but by doing so he lures in brothers who can't swim in it. The stronger brother therefore has a responsibility to stay on the beach.

Christ died for the weaker brother, to save him, and not so that some know-it-all Christian might come along and destroy him by enticing him back into idolatry.

CHRIST IDENTIFIES WITH THE GUY WHO IS WRONG

> But when ye sin so against the brethren, and wound their weak conscience, ye sin against Christ. Wherefore, if meat make my brother to offend, I will eat no flesh while the world standeth, lest I make my brother to offend. (1 Cor. 8:12–13)

So the issue is relationships within the body, and not the liberty of a man with a robust conscience to eat meat from a pagan temple. In short, a man who knows that there is nothing wrong with the meat because Christ is Lord of all, and who then exercises that liberty in a way that wounds a brother with a weak conscience, will find that Christ identifies with the weak brother and not with the strong. Given how Christ died for us while we were still sinners, this should not be surprising. In the dispute between two brothers in the body, Christ sides with the one who is wrong. This is because there is a deeper right than being right.

Paul says that our brother should be more important than our right to eat meat. If that is the choice, as it frequently is, then we should rather become vegetarians than to stumble a brother such that he lapses back into pagan idolatry. This is a very specific caution—Paul is not saying that we must live in such a way as to make absolutely everybody happy. He is saying that we are not to lure someone who is weak into an exercise of liberty that requires strength to handle. Compared to my brother's personal salvation, my personal convenience is nothing.

At the same time, we have to remember and recognize that Paul rebukes believers for submitting to petty legalisms. "Let no man therefore judge you in meat, or in drink . . ." (Col. 2:16). When someone sets himself up as your personal liberty sheriff, and tells you that you must not ever drink alcohol because there are former drunks in the world, your reply must be that this is a dictum that was mysteriously overlooked at Cana.

CHAPTER 9

KIND OF MESSY

> Am I not an apostle? am I not free? have I not seen Jesus Christ our Lord? are not ye my work in the Lord? If I be not an apostle unto others, yet doubtless I am to you: for the seal of mine apostleship are ye in the Lord. (1 Cor. 9:1–2)

The argument in 1 Corinthians now turns to the subject of ministerial support, and Paul begins this discussion by mentioning his office, his apostolic authority. This is the starting point—he asks rhetorically whether he is an apostle. He then adds the ramifications of this. If he is an apostle, then is he not free (to receive support)? That is his statement of the question that this passage addresses in detail.

Paul then goes on to cite two grounds of his apostleship. The first is the qualification of his call and commissioning. Not only did he see Jesus Christ after His resurrection, he also heard Him. Jesus did not appear to him in a silent and mysterious vision—He appeared to him and gave him explicit marching orders. Just as Jesus told the other apostles on the Mount of Olives to disciple the nations, so He told Paul on the Damascus road to disciple the Gentiles (Acts 9:5ff; Acts 22:7ff; Acts 26:15ff). So Paul is a true apostle, commissioned by Christ directly, alongside the other apostles.

But Paul also points to another set of qualifications that authenticate his calling. He points to the Corinthians themselves, indicating the fruit of his ministry with them. Despite all the problems that particular church had (and they were not insignificant), Paul is still pleased to use them as the seal on his ordination papers. Their very existence as a body of believers verified his apostleship. Ministerial authority is therefore personal. Biblical credentials include living, breathing people . . . and how they are doing with the Lord.

It is not a bad idea to supplement biblical standards with, say, educational graduate school standards, but it is a terrible idea to replace biblical standards with such things. While we must always remember that we are evaluating character, not counting rocks, at the same time it is necessary to take personal realities into account. This is why Paul requires a minister's grown children to be faithful

Christians (1 Tim. 3:4–5; Tit. 1:6). If a man cannot disciple his own children, how can he be expected to do a good job with anybody else?

At the same time, it has to be said that those Christians who pay any attention to this elder qualification at all tend to do so with a perfectionistic and jaundiced eye. If a minister has a child who put up a stupid Facebook post, then it is thought by certain particular saints that we have now come to the end of days. For this group, let us remember not only that Paul measured his apostleship with transformed lives, he also made this point by claiming his legacy in a church that had problems with incest, drunkenness at communion, catfight lawsuits between parishioners, and new members who had to be told to stop sleeping with pagan hookers.

Ministerial credentials are therefore personal, transformative, holy . . . and kind of messy.

ALL ABOUT MONEY

> Mine answer to them that do examine me is this, Have we not power to eat and to drink? Have we not power to lead about a sister, a wife, as well as other apostles, and as the brethren of the Lord, and Cephas? Or I only and Barnabas, have not we power to forbear working? (1 Cor. 9:3–6)

Paul then turns to answer a particular charge, one that has been common since the first century (v. 3). That charge is that the ministry is—for the one being criticized—an indoor job with no heavy lifting. In short, it is a cushy job, and those who hold that job down are in fat city, and those providing financial support to them have a right and responsibility to look at them sideways.

Certain people had gotten out the magnifying glass in order to go over Paul's expense account, calling it (of course) responsible stewardship. Paul begins by stating his financial rights, bottom line, and in the verses that follow he will provide the argument for it. Ministers do not run on air. They have the authority to expect food and drink in return for their labors (v. 4). Moreover they have a right to support a family on the strength of what they bring in from the ministry (v. 5). The other apostles, and the brothers of the Lord, and Peter, were all accompanied by "sisters," by their wives. Paul asks the rhetorical question why the tight-fisted approach to ministry budgets applies only to him and to Barnabas (v. 6).

A glance at the North American landscape will reveal that ministers are both overpaid and underpaid. There are ludicrous examples at both ends of that bell curve, but money being the kind of thing it is, there are more who are underpaid than there are those swanking around in television studios. As we resist temptation, our starting point ought to be to guard ourselves in the places where Scripture warns us to guard ourselves. And the consistent warning of Scripture is (overwhelmingly) to make sure you are paying ministers of Christ *enough*. This is particularly the case the more faithful a minister is—this is because a faithful man makes enemies, and enemies frequently arrange for themselves a seat on the budget committee, or they find other ways of attaching costs to his faithfulness. And, everything else being equal, that faithful minister won't talk about it readily. Like the apostle Paul, he would rather have a gun to his head than talk about money.

PAULINE COMMON SENSE

> Who goeth a warfare any time at his own charges? who planteth a vineyard, and eateth not of the fruit thereof? or who feedeth a flock, and eateth not of the milk of the flock? (1 Cor. 9:7)

Paul begins his case with a commonsense observation. He is arguing for a practice that is fully supported by Scripture, as we will see in the following verses, but he begins with an appeal to the very nature of things. He uses three examples—one military and two agricultural.

The military example is an example of hiring and employment. If a soldier is recruited by someone, the expectation is that the "someone" will take care of the expenses. You shouldn't have to bring your own gun. So much is obvious.

The agricultural examples are slightly different. The man planting a vineyard and the man tending a flock are both expected to draw support from their labor directly. A portion of the grapes are his to consume, and a portion of the milk is his to consume.

The application is that a minister should be supported by the field he is working in. Paul will go on to buttress this argument with the teaching of Scripture, but if the Scriptures were silent on the subject, ministers should still be supported better than they frequently are—natural law teaches us this.

THE OX AND THE MUZZLE

> Say I these things as a man? or saith not the law the same also? For it is written in the law of Moses, Thou shalt not muzzle the mouth of the ox that treadeth out the corn. Doth God take care for oxen? Or saith he it altogether for our sakes? For our sakes, no doubt, this is written: that he that ploweth should plow in hope; and that he that thresheth in hope should be partaker of his hope. (1 Cor. 9:8–10)

Paul has argued for this point (on ministerial compensation) from natural law, which he equates with arguing "as a man." He then asks, rhetorically, whether his case is limited to that. He then supplies his own answer, indicating that the law says the same thing.

The law he cites is from Dt. 25:4. Paul cites this passage again in 1 Tim. 5:18. He is very explicit—he says that the law about the treatment of oxen is not really about oxen. It would be a stretch to say that the law excludes oxen, but we really have to say that the primary point of the law is our treatment of other humans. He says that the law was given "altogether" for our sakes. The man who plows should have a share in the profits. The man who threshes should have a share in the profits also. This universal principle is emphatically *not* set aside when talking about ministerial compensation.

There are three things we may take away from this passage. The first is that biblical labor is teleological, and the *telos* is the fruit of the labor. Laboring without a mind for the results is not disinterested and noble; it is short-sighted and stupid. The one who labors should labor in hope. The second is that this whole principle presupposes some form of essential ownership. All forms of collective ownership—socialism and the like—are out. But last, this does not make every man an island. The apostle uses the word partaker here when talking about someone else in the production chain. The one who threshes should be a partaker together with the one who plows. They cooperate together, and they share in the profits.

A HOT LITTLE RED SARKI-CAR

> If we have sown unto you spiritual things, is it a great thing if we shall reap your carnal things? If others be partakers of this power over you, are not we rather? Nevertheless we have not used this power; but suffer all things, lest we should hinder the gospel of Christ. (1 Cor. 9:11–12)

So the principle is plainly stated. Those who sow into the ground of people's spiritual lives should be able to expect financial support for their labors in return. Paul asks "is it a great thing?"—meaning that it shouldn't be considered a big deal when it happens. It should be taken as part of the ordinary course of events. Paul teaches here that a spiritual investment in a spiritual ministry ought to have a *carnal* return. The word he uses is *sarkika*—fleshly.

If others exercise this claim over the Corinthians (as other teachers were apparently doing), Paul wonders why he and his companions do not have even more of a claim. This is the way it goes. Those who have a deeper claim along with a deeper understanding forgo the claim. Those with a legitimate claim along with a more superficial understanding demand their payment—here's the verse, what's the problem?

Paul goes on to point out that the reason he was not being paid at the same levels as those with a lesser claim was because he knew that there was a deeper right than being right. There was a more important point than the point of the pen signing the paycheck. Paul knew that a minister can receive something that is his due, and receive it in such a way as to hinder the work he was appointed to do. Rather than do that, Paul says that he would put up with all kinds of indignities and insults rather than create (by means of a *legitimate* demand) a problem for the progress of the gospel. He is referring to the kind of problem that arises in the minds of those you will never have a chance to explain it to.

Would it be a sin for a minister to take a hefty pay raise he just got and buy a hot little red convertible sports car—his *sarki-car*—and then have his wife dye her hair a white kind of platinum, and then drive around the church parking lot with the top down? Is that a sin? The Bible says nothing about it being a sin one way or the other, but it would sure be stupid. Would it get in the way of the gospel? To ask the question is to answer it.

EVEN SO

> Do ye not know that they which minister about holy things live of the things of the temple? and they which wait at the altar are partakers with the altar? Even so

hath the Lord ordained that they which preach the gospel should live of the gospel. (1 Cor. 9:13–14)

Thus far Paul has argued that natural law requires a just payment for ministers, and that an argument by analogy from the Old Testament law requires it. If the ox should not be muzzled in his work, how much less should a minister of the gospel be muzzled in his?

At this place in his argument, Paul steps it up, making it as strong as he can make it. The word translated "ordained" here is *diatasso*. Various translations give us the force of it—"commanded" (NKJV and ESV) and "directed" (NASB). In any case, it is not that the Lord is leaving us without *authoritative* direction on how we should pay our ministers. And how is that? The answer is by means of the tithe. A tithe-based support is a *commanded* support. Everything is just suggestion, juiced by inspiration, surrounded by flowery language.

We see this in the words at the beginning of verse 14—even so. *Kai houtos*, even so, in the same way as, *in the same manner*. Christian ministers should be paid in the same manner as old covenant ministers were paid, and that was by means of the tithe. The system which enabled the ministers of the temple and altar to live was a system of tithing. Do it that way, Paul says. This makes good sense because the prophet Isaiah predicted that in the days to come, the Gentiles would worship the Lord, calling Him by a new name (Isa. 62:2), and in that day God would call priests and Levites "out of all nations" (Isa. 66:20–21). With God having called these priests and Levites out, Paul teaches us here that they should be paid in much the same way that the older priests and Levites were.

PAULINE BRAGGING RIGHTS

> But I have used none of these things: neither have I written these things, that it should be so done unto me: for it were better for me to die, than that any man should make my glorying void. (1 Cor. 9:15)

So Paul has been going on and on about money, and since I am commenting on 1 Corinthians verse by verse, so have I been. In fact, we have been harping on this point so much (Paul and I) that one begins to suspect an ulterior motive. It is sort of like when the minister starts preaching "Stewardship Sunday" messages every third week or so—one begins to wonder if the old budget is having any difficulties.

No, that is not the issue. Paul knows that he is ministering among sinful men, and he knows the ranks of the ministers are also filled up with sinful men. There is the sin that doesn't want to give, and there is the sin that just wants to take. He knows that people naturally begrudge giving money to ministers who are well worth it—and whose first reasonable paycheck will come at the last day in front of all the angels—and he knows that plenty of ministers who are not worth a thin spiritual dime have taken full advantage of the flock—shepherds who feed only themselves. The problem with Brother Love's Old Time Holiness Hour is not the pay he gets—it is the slipshod nature of his work.

This is why Paul fights for the principle that insists that good and godly ministers should be paid well, and why he fights also for the (equally important) principle that defines good and godly ministers as those who are willing to forego what is their due for the sake of the gospel, for the sake of the mission. That foundational reality comes to the front in this verse.

Paul says that there are certain financial prerogatives that he refused to draw on. He had an account that he refused to open. Moreover, he did not teach the Corinthians about the existence of this account as a sneaky and surreptitious way of tricking *them* into opening it for him. He has not taken advantage of his right, and he makes that point first—"I have used none of these things." And he did not teach on it in order that it should "be so done unto me." He did not write this letter with one eye on the budget meeting that was coming up. Not only does he make this point, he glories in it. He would rather die than have any money come to him in a way that would deprive him of these bragging rights.

But it is crucial that we get this right because we are so prone to slip off the point in either direction. Some ministers say that if they claim the right and privilege to the money, then they must get the money necessarily. Others say that since it is a disgrace for a minister to make all that money, they must not have the right to it. Robbing ministers is to them an act of justice, instead of what Paul would call it, an act of sacrificial love.

So Paul rejects both options—if Paul were paid like a televangelist, we shouldn't begrudge a penny of it. He would be worth it all. And because he is the kind of man who would deserve it, we find out that he is the kind of man who would refuse every penny of it, rather than jeopardize the mission.

Paul feels strongly on the point. He would rather die than to give it up. And a good word to ministers here would be to imitate him as he imitates Christ. Unless, of course, ministerial pay has not gotten in the way of the mission since A.D. 64, when the good apostle died.

FIRE IN HIS BONES

> For though I preach the gospel, I have nothing to glory of: for necessity is laid upon me; yea, woe is unto me, if I preach not the gospel! For if I do this thing willingly, I have a reward: but if against my will, a dispensation of the gospel is committed unto me. (1 Cor. 9:16–17)

Jeremiah realized at one point that whenever he opened his mouth, he got into trouble. So he resolved to shut up . . . but when he did that, he discovered fire in his bones, fire that wouldn't let him keep quiet (Jer. 20:9). Paul felt himself similarly constrained.

He preaches the gospel, but gets no glory from that because whether he feels like preaching or not, he has the assignment anyway. Necessity is "laid upon" him. If he revolts against his assignment (something that the passage indicates may have happened from time to time), God does not remove the stewardship (*oikonomia*) that was entrusted to him. He talks about the nature of the reward he has for willing service in the verses coming up, but simply notes here that if he serves willingly he has a reward coming.

The point he is making is that he is not in it for the money, and he is not in it for the rewards he might get. He is in it because God threw him in it. It is worth remembering that in the ten minutes prior to his apostolic call, he had been breathing threats and murder against the followers of Christ.

A DEEPER RECOMPENSE

> What is my reward then? Verily that, when I preach the gospel, I may make the gospel of Christ without charge, that I abuse not my power in the gospel. (1 Cor. 9:18)

In short, the apostle's reward is foregoing the reward. Not only is there a deeper right than being right, there is a deeper recompense than being recompensed. He doesn't want to preach the gospel in a venue that requires him to sell tickets for it. If the message is free, then it is a great privilege to proclaim that free grace in a way that resembles the grace itself.

But it is important to note that Paul is assuming that if the gospel came *"with* a charge," this would be a power he had in the gospel. This power is one that he is intent on not *abusing*, but it is a power nonetheless. The plowman plows with a hope of the harvest, and if Paul foregoes payment it is only because he is intent on plowing deeper. And that means a fuller harvest, when the time is right.

WHEN MORE GRAIN WAS GOLDEN

> For though I be free from all men, yet have I made myself servant unto all, that I might gain the more. (1 Cor. 9:19)

Here he states the principle, and in the verses following Paul gives three examples of how he applied the principle. He became as a Jew (v. 20), he became as one apart from the law (v. 21), and he became weak (v. 22). The principle is that he imitated the Lord Jesus, who became like us in our lowly state in order to bring us salvation. Not only did he imitate the Lord, he imitated the Lord in the freedom he had to *not* do it.

If God owed us our salvation, it wouldn't be by grace. Paul was not a church planter under constraint from the demands of those who would be blessed by it; he says emphatically that he is "free from all men." What moved him then? He was constrained by the promise of an abundant harvest, a harvest that was going to stagger the imagination. He gave himself away so that he "might gain the more."

He had a deep insight into the very nature of the world. God has built planting and harvesting right into the fabric of all things, and Paul had learned to see his life as seed, and to long for the time when more grain was golden than any man ever thought of.

UNDER THE LAW OF CHRIST

> And unto the Jews I became as a Jew, that I might gain the Jews; to them that are under the law, as under the law, that I might gain them that are under the law; To them that are without the law, as without law, (being not without law to God, but under the law to Christ,) that I might gain them that are without law. (1 Cor. 9:20–21)

Paul here states his practice of cultural accommodation, both with Jews and with Gentiles. When ministering to Jews, when ministering to those "under the law," he fit himself to their condition. To the Gentiles, who lived outside the restrictions of Torah, Paul lived that way himself, so as not to put any unnecessary obstacle between the Jews and Christ, or between the Gentiles and Christ. In other word, he didn't bring a BLT to the synagogue lunch, and he didn't turn down a BLT at the country club.

This should not be read as lawlessness, but rather submission to a higher law, the law of Christ. The Torah was from God originally, but now that the building was up, it was time for the scaffolding to come down. Paul living lawfully before God, under the law of Christ, should be seen here as the building. A rejection of temporary scaffolding is not a rejection of the building, particularly when his task was that of gathering living stones for the building from the Jewish and Gentile quarries both.

ALL AND SOME

> To the weak became I as weak, that I might gain the weak: I am made all things to all men, that I might by all means save some. (1 Cor. 9:22)

We see here Paul's driving zeal for evangelism. He has just finished saying that he was willing to be a Jew for the sake of the Jews and play the part of someone "without law" to those who were outside the law. He did this, not as a lawless one, but as one under the law of Christ. Here he applies the same principle to another category—to those who are weak. He doesn't specify what sort of weakness, but the range of the word includes feebleness, sickness, or impotence. Whatever it is, it would not be the sort of thing that someone of Paul's caliber would usually aspire to. He was willing to become "as weak" in order to gain the weak.

This is an extreme application of the principle, and Paul makes it clear that it is, evangelistically speaking, a principle of broad application. He is willing, he says, to be made all things to all men so that by all means he might save some. This is quite striking—all, all, all, some. All things to all men so that by all means he might save some. He is not an each and every universalist. He knows that some will be saved and some will not be. But if some are not saved, it will not be because of a refusal on Paul's part to identify with them—whether Jew or Gentile, or weak or not.

One other note. His motivation here is a zeal for the gospel, and not a pathetic yearning in his own ego to be with all the rich and swanky people, or the cool kids with the skateboards. He wants to win the people he identifies with to Christ. He is not looking for a group of people who are cool enough to win him from Christ.

GOSPEL PARTAKING

> And this I do for the gospel's sake, that I might be partaker thereof with you. (1 Cor. 9:23)

Paul has made the particular sacrifices he has just finished mentioning with a particular end in mind. He was willing to be Jewish with the Jews, not under the law for those not under the law, and weak with those who were weak. He was willing to do anything (within the constraints created by the law of Christ) in order to save some of God's elect. He did all this, he says here, for the gospel's sake.

What is meant by that phrase "for the gospel's sake"? Paul explains it in the next phrase—"that I might be partaker thereof with you." The gospel is not an abstraction in the sky. The gospel is the message of God's truth intended to bring us into fellowship with God again, and with one another. This fellowship is more than just friendly chatting in the coffee and donut time after church. The word here is a strong one—the gospel enables us to be partakers of one another. Among others, it enables us to become partakers together with Jews, Gentiles, and the weak, along with everybody else.

A STRANGE RACE INDEED

> Know ye not that they which run in a race run all, but one receiveth the prize? So run, that ye may obtain. (1 Cor. 9:24)

This verse can only be understood as high paradox. Paul has just finished saying that he becomes as a Jew to let the Jews go first, and he becomes like one without the law to let those without the law go first. He becomes weak, so that the weak might be gained. He wants the weak to go ahead of him—they are more important to him than he is. He does all this for the sake of the gospel, so that they can all partake together. So, he wants them all to go ahead of him, and he also wants all of them to arrive together.

And he does this because only one takes the prize, only one national anthem is played, only one gold medal is handed out, and Paul wants to run in such a way as to be that one who wins that prize. Moreover, he tells the Corinthians that they should each run with that same goal in mind.

The only conclusion we can draw is that this is a very strange race indeed, one in which the last are first.

MEANS AND ENDS

> And every man that striveth for the mastery is temperate in all things. Now they do it to obtain a corruptible crown; but we an incorruptible. I therefore so run, not as uncertainly; so fight I, not as one that beateth the air: But I keep under my body, and bring it into subjection: lest that by any means, when I have preached to others, I myself should be a castaway. (1 Cor. 9:25–27)

Paul sees himself in training, and not for a contest that will give him a temporary gold, silver, or bronze medal. He is in it for an incorruptible crown, a crown that cannot be taken away or lost. Although the ends are dissimilar, the regime of training is similar. Paul is temperate in all things, just as a runner who is striving "for mastery" is temperate in all things.

When Paul says he runs, but not "uncertainly," he is saying that he is focused. And his boxing is not shadow boxing, but he has a real opponent, which is his body (*soma*). He pummels his body, and makes it his slave. The stakes are high—he does not want to be the one who preached an incorruptible crown to others, only to fall short of it himself. Bringing salvation to others was the race he was assigned to run as he was given the gift of salvation himself.

Those who worry that Paul's nervous reference to himself becoming a castaway is somehow inconsistent with his high theology of salvation expressed elsewhere (e.g., Rom. 8:33–39) are those who don't have a robust theology of means and ends. Paul knew that they were all going to survive the storm they were in (Acts 27:24), and he also knew that if the sailors got away in their boat they weren't going to survive it (Acts 27:31). He also knew that if he let his body get the upper hand, he was going to be lost.

CHAPTER 10

GNOSTICS AND SACRAMENTS

> Moreover, brethren, I would not that ye should be ignorant, how that all our fathers were under the cloud, and all passed through the sea; and were all baptized unto Moses in the cloud and in the sea; and did all eat the same spiritual meat; and did all drink the same spiritual drink: for they drank of that spiritual Rock that followed them: and that Rock was Christ" (1 Cor. 10:1–4).

For many evangelical Christians, we have come to a section of Corinthians that is very challenging indeed. This is because we have a tendency to draw contrasts between the

Old and New Testaments in the very places where the New Testament draws parallels.

We can begin with the fact that Paul calls the Gentile Corinthian believers *brothers,* and in the next breath tells them that "our *fathers*" passed through the sea. Paul, a Jew, identifies with them, and immediately draws a connection between them and the fathers of Israel.

The second thing is that it was the Corinthians who had started to put on airs, saying that they had spiritual privileges that the Jews did not have. Paul refutes this idea sharply, telling them that the Jews were baptized also, the Jews had a spiritual food also, and that the Jews had spiritual drink also. The trajectory of this line of thought finishes in the next verse. God was displeased with them anyway (v. 5), and the implication is that He could just as easily be displeased with the Corinthians (v. 6). Take heed—the root supports you, not the other way around.

The third thing is that being baptized into *Moses* gave the Jews access to *Christ.* Their baptism was Mosaic, and their sacramental drink was Christ. The Mosaic economy was an administration of the covenant of grace, as the Westminster Confession puts it (Chapter VII).

And then last, it is plain from this account that Scripture has a category of objective partaking of the covenant. Someone can partake of Christ objectively (in a true sacrament) without partaking of Him subjectively (in true regeneration). The idolaters of verse 7 were the communicants of verses 3–4. But the fact that it is possible does not make it okay. But the fact that it is possible does mean—follow me closely—that it is not impossible.

So Pauline theology here refutes two common mistakes. The first, the Gnostic Calvinist evangelical, cannot account for how people could actually drink Christ and still fall under God's displeasure as idolaters. The second, the formalist sacramentard, cannot account for how they could drink Christ and actually fall under judgment.

EVANGELICAL AND REFORMED EYES

> But with many of them God was not well pleased: for they were overthrown in the wilderness. Now these things were our examples, to the intent we should not lust after evil things, as they also lusted. (1 Cor. 10:5–6)

We have seen that the New Testament draws parallels between Christians of the New Testament and Jews of the Old. There are obviously a number of discontinuities between the covenants, described at length in the New Testament elsewhere, but they are not discontinuities across the board, and they are not discontinuities placed where incipient Marcionites like to place them.

On the issues of sacramental partaking of Christ and the possibility of covenantal apostasy, we find continuity between the covenants. The Israelites who fell in the wilderness under the displeasure of God were a type of judgment, and they were among those who drank from the Rock that was Christ. They had spiritual food and drink in the wilderness, just like the Corinthians had spiritual food and drink in the Supper, but what happened to them was designed as a warning or an example to new covenant believers.

Let us put the question in the simplest possible terms. Was it possible for an Old Testament Israelite to drink from the Rock of Christ, and subsequently fall under the displeasure of God in the wilderness, and to do so as a warning to new covenant Christians? The answer is *yes*.

If a particular systematic theology cannot incorporate this reality, then I would suggest that it is time for a new systematic theology. And lest anyone try to defend against this necessity by using scare words like Arminian and sacramentalist, it is important to note that there is a way of understanding Paul's teaching here that is both evangelical and Reformed. In fact, as we work through this chapter it will become apparent that the only way to understand the full spectrum is by looking at it with evangelical and Reformed eyes.

FOUR WARNINGS

> Neither be ye idolaters, as were some of them; as it is written, The people sat down to eat and drink, and rose up to play. Neither let us commit fornication, as some of them committed, and fell in one day three and twenty thousand. Neither let us tempt Christ, as some of them also tempted, and were destroyed of serpents. Neither murmur ye, as some of them also murmured, and were destroyed of the destroyer. (1 Cor. 10:7–10)

Paul gives the Corinthian Christians four warning examples, bookended with the reminder that the wilderness period of the Israelites served as an example (vv. 6, 11) for those on whom the ends of the ages had come. The four episodes were the festival to Yahweh centered on the worship of a golden calf (Ex. 32:6). There was the plague at Baal-Peor because of the sexual enticements suggested by Balaam (Num. 31:16). The revolt over food and drink was followed by a judgment of biting serpents (Num. 21:5–6). The fourth incident probably refers to the episode with Korah (Num. 16).

The sins of God's people in these incidents were syncretistic and licentious worship, fornication, tempting Christ by revolting against authority, and murmuring. All these sins, Paul warns, were well within the reach of the Christians at Corinth. As you read through the admonitions to the church there, you can find difficulties in each one of these areas.

So we see it is not the case that the distinction between the Israelites in the wilderness and the Christians in the new covenant rests in the inability of the latter to commit these sins. No, the whole account of the wilderness was written down precisely so that Christians would know what not to do. It follows then that members of the new covenant can "tempt Christ."

THIRD CHAPTER OF JUDGES

> Now all these things happened unto them for ensamples: and they are written for our admonition, upon whom the ends of the world are come. (1 Cor. 10:11)

We have already seen the parallels between Old Testament saints and New Testament saints. But in this verse we see an even closer parallel, one between the Old Testament saints in the wilderness and the New Testament saints in the wilderness. Israel's wandering in the wilderness for forty years was a type, and the first generation of Christians were the antitype. The Israelite experience in the wilderness was not a detached and timeless truth (although it does have timeless applications). It was written, Paul says, for *our* admonition. Whose admonition? For those upon whom the ends of the ages had come. That would refer to the Christians in the wilderness, waiting for the invasion of the world to commence.

Between the Exodus and the invasion of Canaan were forty years. Between the Exodus of Jesus and the destruction of Jerusalem were forty years. The leadership of Moses was established during that time, as was the leadership of the apostles. God's Torah was given during the forty years, and the New Testament was given to Christians during an equivalent period. Challenges to God's leadership were mounted in both times. And, as we see here, God's people were tempted to tempt Christ, and the Corinthians were told to withstand that temptation because they were on the brink of a new age. That happened in A.D. 70, when the old order collapsed, and the Church was commanded to fan out throughout the entire world.

Of course, fulfilling the Great Commission can be kind of messy. I figure we are about in the third chapter of Judges. No need for perfectionism—just faithfulness.

THEOLOGICALLY SPEAKING YOU STAND

> Wherefore let him that thinketh he standeth take heed lest he fall. (1 Cor. 10:12)

This short verse quite obviously applies to the universal temptation to pride. We know that pride goes before destruction, and a haughty spirit before a fall (Prov. 16:18). This is a truth that is always good to remember.

But there is a more particular meaning as well—there is a theological caution here. The Corinthians believers had fallen into the mistaken notion that they somehow occupied a place in the covenant that was radically different in kind from the place occupied by the Israelites in the wilderness. They were proud over their privileges over the Jews—and pointed to baptism, for example, and to the spiritual food that was supplied to them in the Supper. But Paul replies bluntly to them that they had *nothing* that Israelites in the wilderness did not also have. They had baptism too (vv. 1–2), and they had spiritual food and spiritual drink (vv. 3–4). They even had Christ Himself (v. 4). And yet, that did not keep the bodies of many of the Israelites from falling under the judgment of God (v. 5).

So this caution that Paul gives us here is a caution for those who would use false theological assumptions to buttress their pride. We know that God's election is sure, and cannot be altered. But covenantal standing is a different matter. Beware lest the two are somehow confounded—let him who thinks he stands in the covenant beware lest he fall away from the covenant.

IDOLATRY EVERYWHERE

> There hath no temptation taken you but such as is common to man: but God is faithful, who will not suffer you to be tempted above that ye are able; but will with the temptation also make a way to escape, that ye

> may be able to bear it. Wherefore, my dearly beloved, flee from idolatry. (1 Cor. 10:13–14)

It is common to take verse 13 as a statement that whatever temptation you might be going through, don't worry, other folks have gone through that one too. Not only have others experienced the temptation also, but God is versatile and is able to deliver you from whatever it is. But the "common to man" appears to be saying something else—which is that all temptations reduce to one common denominator. Right after Paul says this, and says that God will provide a way of escape, he follows it up in the next verse by telling the Corinthians to flee from idolatry. This appears to be the root sin; this is the common-to-man failing. Wherever we go, whatever we do, we are going to be confronted with the temptation to idolatry.

The examples given earlier in this chapter (vv. 6–10) are all examples that reduce to idolatry, which is placing a created thing in the spot that only the uncreated God should occupy. Idolatry is the attempt to get from a finite thing what only the infinite can supply. These sins are lust, idolatry proper, fornication, tempting Christ, and murmuring. All of them rest upon an idolatrous foundation.

This means that whenever God makes a way of escape, and you avail yourself of it, you are following the charge of verse 14, and are fleeing from idolatry.

ARMED AGAINST IDOLATRY

> I speak as to wise men; judge ye what I say. (1 Cor. 10:15)

This cryptic statement is the segue between Paul's discussion of the Israelites failures in the wilderness (given as examples to new covenant Christians), and his detailed theological discussion of the meaning of the Lord's Supper. He says that he is speaking to wise men, and he wants them to evaluate or judge what he says. We need to remember Paul's earlier rejection in this letter of a particular kind of wisdom—the wisdom of this world will be no good at all.

There are many things that could be said here, but I will content myself with simply two. The first is that believers must go into their celebrations of the Lord's Supper armed and equipped against the temptation to idolatry. The second thing is that we live in a world where covenantal partaking happens in many different ways. Paul says here that faithful believers have *koinonia* with the blood and body of Jesus Christ (v. 16). He says that the Israelites were partakers of the *koinonia* sacrifices at the altar (v. 18). And he says that, despite the idols not being anything, those who sacrifice there have *koinonia* with devils (v. 21). *Koinonia* fellowship is everywhere, which is why we always have to be prepared to fight idolatry.

BREAKING AND BLESSING

> The cup of blessing which we bless, is it not the communion of the blood of Christ? The bread which we break, is it not the communion of the body of Christ?
> (1 Cor. 10:16)

We are coming into a stretch of Paul's letter to the Corinthians which is dense and rich. On top of this, it is even more freighted with meaning because of the debates and controversies throughout Church history over "what happens" when the Supper is observed. We should limit our discussion of what happens to what the text says—which is less than some want, and a great deal more than many others want. We should not allow ourselves to have a hidden set of metaphysical assumptions dictate to us what needs to be happening. We should limit ourselves here to "what" questions, which can be answered from the text, and not get into the metaphysical "hows," which cannot be.

In this verse, we perform two actions, one toward the cup, which is that of blessing, and one toward the bread, which is that of breaking. This cup of blessing, blessed by us, is the *koinonia* of the blood of Christ. This bread, broken by us, is the *koinonia* of the body of Christ. From this we may conclude two important actions that are necessary in the Supper, those of blessing and breaking. The consequence is that we partake, commune, participate in, fellowship in, the blood and body of Jesus. This is the what. The partaking is stronger than simply remembering. At the same time, the partaking is covenantal and sacramental, not a miraculous zapping of essences. The same kind of partaking was going on in the Old Testament sacrifices (v. 18), and the same kind of thing was actually happening in the idolatrous worship of devils (v. 20). This partaking happens because of how the world was created, and not because of some wizardry that changed the bread and wine into something else.

MYSTERIOUS AND SACRAMENTAL MEANS

> For we being many are one bread, and one body: for we are all partakers of that one bread. (1 Cor. 10:17)

As we all are fragmented pieces of bread, yet we are all portions of one loaf. In the sacrament of the Lord's Supper, one loaf is broken into many fragments so that many fragments may be united into one loaf. This is a deep pattern that God loves to use. He took Adam and broke him in two in order that He might take those two and unite them into one. The second one was richer and deeper than the previous unitary one. Then one of those two conceived, and the one became two, and when he grew up and took a wife, the two became one.

We have something similar happening in the Supper. The Lord's body was broken, just as Adam's was. When His body was broken, a bride was formed out of His side (John 19:34–35). That one bride, that one loaf, is then broken, but broken in such a way as to create a deeper, richer, much more textured unity among the people. The people are the loaf, the people are the smaller fragments, and the people are a loaf again. The Holy Spirit is growing us up into a perfect man by this mysterious and sacramental means.

SACRAMENTALS

> Behold Israel after the flesh: are not they which eat of the sacrifices partakers of the altar? (1 Cor. 10:18)

Paul here points to a covenantal reality that undoes quite a few metaphysical theories about the sacraments. What is happening in the Lord's Supper is not a one-off situation. It happened to Israelites "after the flesh" in the time of the old covenant. The same thing happened to pagan worshipers when they sacrificed (v. 20), resulting in fellowship with devils.

This is a covenantal connection, and it is the way the world is built to work. We have only two appointed sacraments in the Christian faith (baptism and the Lord's Supper), but nevertheless the world is jammed full of "sacramentals." Those sacramentals may be participated in by faith, or they may be seized in rebellion, and they remain what they are regardless. A man may become one flesh with his wife (Eph. 5:31), but if it is with a hooker, the unity of flesh still happens (1 Cor. 6:16). One man communes with Yahweh at His altar by eating part of a roast, and another man communes with demons by eating the same part of the roast from another cow, and this all happens without any changes whatever happening to the meat (1 Cor. 10:28). The earth is the Lord's and the fullness thereof. The meat is not demon-possessed, and the meat doesn't have Yahweh in it. We participate in the world sacramentally, which is to say, we do so by faith.

So whatever was happening when a man sacrificed to Aphrodite and slept with one of her priestesses, it was not anything like consubstantiation, transubstantiation, or mere memorialism. Nothing was happening to internal essences while leaving the external accidents intact. Neither was it a mere sign pointing to something else happening someplace else entirely. It really was fellowship with devils. And whatever happened when a man brought a peace offering in ancient Israel, it was not the meat of the sacrifice turning into another substance. Nevertheless, that man was truly becoming a partaker of the altar.

This kind of covenantal participation does not require a priest, or special magic words. Ours is a covenantal participation at one of two possible tables, and we do so by virtue of simply being alive in this world. The only question is where we are partaking by faith, not whether we are.

GODS AND DEVILS

> What say I then? that the idol is any thing, or that which is offered in sacrifice to idols is any thing? But I say, that the things which the Gentiles sacrifice, they sacrifice to devils, and not to God: and I would not that ye should have fellowship with devils. (1 Cor. 10:19–20)

Paul insists that, on one level, nothing is happening in idol worship. On another level, a great deal is happening—devil worship is happening. Ancient paganism was not simple superstition at the center. In other words, there were spiritual realities at the center—diabolical, but real for all that. What the ancients called gods and goddesses, the Bible called devils. As we saw a few chapters prior to this, Paul does acknowledge the existence of "gods many, and lords many" (1 Cor. 8:5). But their existence was not at the top of some pantheon. There is only one Creator God, and all other beings are on this side of the Creator/creature divide.

This is clearly seen in the episode at Philippi, where Paul cast out a fortune-telling demon from a girl (Acts 16:18). Literally she had what Luke called the spirit of a python, which meant that she was a devotee of the god Apollo. What the pagans saw as "a god," the believers saw as a devil. Neither of them saw it as empty tomfoolery.

There are two rival sacrificial systems in the world, that of Christ and that of devils. Devils are accusers, and so the resultant bloodshed is always human blood, and it must be offered repeatedly. It is a system that devours its worshipers, as opposed to the Christian faith, which feeds them. The blood shed by Christ was human blood, but it was shed by one who was absolutely free from the spirit of accusation, which meant that He was able to break condemnation's back. In the meantime, these two rival sacrifices each have their own fellowship meals, and their own patterns of *koinonia*.

There are two tables then. There is a table of condemnation and a table of no condemnation. Believers are summoned to eat at the latter, and to refrain from turning it into a table of condemnation.

ONE INSTEAD OF TWO

> Ye cannot drink the cup of the Lord, and the cup of devils: ye cannot be partakers of the Lord's table, and of the table of devils. Do we provoke the Lord to jealousy? are we stronger than he? (1 Cor. 10:21–22)

At the very beginning, the Lord established the antithesis in the world between the seed of the woman and the seed of the serpent. We see the same reality spoken of here. There are only two tables in the world—God's, and that of the devils. God says that it must be one or the other, and we find this radical necessity of choice too confining. Many want to have it both ways, and to be able to partake from both tables. But God forbids it, and regards all such attempts to eat from both tables as a provocation to His jealousy. Jealousy, we must never forget, is a divine attribute. His name is Jealous (Ex. 34:14), and His strength is unlimited. Why, Paul asks, would we pick a fight with Him?

This is the central temptation that unbelieving man has—he wants to say one where God has said *two*.

CRUCIAL CONTEXT

> All things are lawful for me, but all things are not expedient: all things are lawful for me, but all things edify not. (1 Cor. 10:23)

There are verses where the surrounding context does not matter as much in the reading of the verse, and there are verses where the surrounding context matters a great deal. The phrase "all things" is qualified in context, but is unqualified within the confines of the verse. Apart from context, this passage appears to urge us on to the higher grace of antinomianism. But in context, Paul is talking about a particular set of behaviors—eating meat offered to pagan idols.

He is talking about particular cases of conscience. He is not talking here about, say, fornication, drunkenness, or extortion, as we can readily see by flipping back a few pages (1 Cor. 5:11). Here is a paraphrase of the passage, tailored so that it cannot be made to stand alone. "All the things we are talking about are lawful for me, but they are not expedient. All of those things are lawful, as I said, but doing them won't help you edify your brother."

NOT SEEKING OUR OWN

> Let no man seek his own, but every man another's wealth. Whatsoever is sold in the shambles, that eat, asking no question for conscience sake: For the earth is the Lord's, and the fulness thereof. (1 Cor. 10:24–26)

In this section, Paul mentions a principle that he will repeat again in a moment—which is that the whole earth belongs to God. God not only owns the earth, He owns the fullness of it. This has various applications, and the first one is that each man has his own, and God gives us our own so that we might not seek it. Rather than privilege our own persons or property, we are to use whatever we have in order to seek out a blessing for others.

In this instance, we seek what is best for others by being considerate. We don't have to worry about the history of the meat we purchased in the shambles (meat market) because whatever that history was, the meat is not demon-possessed. The earth is the Lord's, and that includes meat that hours before was on the altar of a pagan deity. There is nothing wrong with the meat—but we might still wrong our brother by how we go about enjoying the meat. The earth is the Lord's, and He tells us that all things are clean. The earth is the Lord's, and He tells us to put our brother first, before ourselves.

LOVE AND LIBERTY

> If any of them that believe not bid you to a feast, and ye be disposed to go; whatsoever is set before you, eat, asking no question for conscience sake. But if any man say unto you, This is offered in sacrifice unto idols, eat not for his sake that shewed it, and for conscience sake: for the earth is the Lord's, and the fulness thereof: Conscience, I say, not thine own, but of the other: for why is my liberty judged of another man's conscience? (1 Cor. 10:27–29)

So Paul gives us a little scenario to help us understand how love and the conscience of others should intersect. He presupposes first that a pagan invites you to a dinner party, and he makes it clear that it is lawful to go if you want to. When you go, you have no responsibility to trace the history of the food. Just eat—your conscience should be untroubled by whether or not the meat on the platter had been offered up to Aphrodite earlier in the week. That should be a matter of indifference to you.

But if you are minding your own business, eating the food with gratitude, and somebody else comes along and says, "Oh, no! That came from the temple of Aphrodite!" you should then refrain. You refrain for the sake of his conscience, not your own. Your own conscience knows that the meat is not demon-possessed. Paul here repeats his refrain that the earth is the Lord's, and all its fullness. Paul repeats himself to make it clear—you are refraining for conscience, but not your own conscience. If you were alone, it would be perfectly fine to eat the meat. My *liberty* is not constrained by his conscience, but my *love* is. Because I refrain for his sake out of love, my liberty is not at all chafed.

There are several modern areas of application. First, note that Paul does not care about the history of the food chain for any *moral* reasons. We are not contaminated spiritually by food that has been in a pagan temple, or in a chicken barn, or grown on a plantation owned by an evil corporation. The history of food can have something to do with salmonella, sure enough, but it has nothing whatever to do with "ethical" eating.

But if your brother comes to you with a concern about that history, you have a two-fold task. One is to not surrender the doctrine that the earth is the Lord's, and the other is to love your brother. Sometimes loving him means you must refrain from eating, as here. Other times it means that you must love him by absolutely refusing to cooperate with his false scruples (Col. 2:16, 20–21). Life is hard. Love the Lord, love His material creation, all of it, and love your brother.

NO ETHEREAL PIOUS GLOW

> For if I by grace be a partaker, why am I evil spoken of for that for which I give thanks? Whether therefore ye eat, or drink, or whatsoever ye do, do all to the glory of God. (1 Cor. 10:30–31)

Paul now moves from the particular situation that the Corinthian Christians faced to an appeal to the general principle that applies to all Christians everywhere, and at all times.

If God has not specifically prohibited something, like a quart of rum in fifteen minutes, then it is lawful to partake of it, whenever that partaking is considered in isolation. In this sense, we can ask whether "eating meat offered to idols" is a sin, or "drinking alcohol," or listening to rock music. All things are lawful, but not all things are necessary.

But when such actions are considered in context, there are two other factors that must be considered when determining whether the action is sinful or not. Those two factors are motives and relationships. Paul says here that the motive for partaking (free from condemnation) must be thanksgiving. If you are giving thanks for whatever it is you are partaking of, then there can be no condemnation for it (v. 30). Is it a sin to eat or drink that? Well, did you say grace over it? This is related to the motive mentioned in the next verse, which is the glory of God (v. 31).

The glory of God is not minimized or insulted when it is brought into our menu choices. God can truly be glorified, and expects to be, down to the last French fry. Doing everything to the glory of God is the basic Pauline impulse, and is the foundation for all true Kuyperianism. It does not mean walking two inches above the floor with spooky music in the background, and with an ethereal pious glow on your face. It means a life suffused with love and gratitude.

The second great factor has to do with whether your liberty is a point of stumbling for others. This has been addressed at length earlier in the chapter, and will be mentioned again in the next verse (v. 32).

ALL THINGS TO ALL MEN

> Give none offense, neither to the Jews, nor to the Gentiles, nor to the church of God: Even as I please

all men in all things, not seeking mine own profit, but the profit of many, that they may be saved. (1 Cor. 10:32–33).

We should start with the goal. Paul is seeking the salvation of many men; he is not playing for small change. Since they are the point of the mission, the one on the mission subordinates his own interests to the task. He seeks to please all men, and denies himself the pleasure of seeking his own profit, because he bends all his efforts toward this end.

The "all men" here encompasses all kinds—Jews, Gentiles, not to mention members of the Church. This ties in with the point of his previous discussion. He is talking about cultural identity markers—dietary issues, ceremonial practices, and so on. When we are on their turf, we are to behave in a respectful way. No one should be able to say that we are being flamboyant and obnoxious for the sake of being obnoxious. You don't take your BLT into the synagogue. You don't swing your liberty around on the end of a rope.

At the same time, Paul says elsewhere that we should be at peace with all men so far as it depends upon us. This requirement to not give offense to Jews, Gentiles, or Christians is not an absolute. Obedience is absolute, but it is to God, and not to my own preferences. My own preferences must give way to the urgency of winning all kinds of men to Christ.

CHAPTER 11

MOONS AND SUN

> Be ye followers of me, even as I also am of Christ. Now I praise you, brethren, that ye remember me in all things, and keep the ordinances, as I delivered them to you. (1 Cor. 11:1–2)

Paul mentions a common biblical theme here, which is that we learn by imitation. The things we really know how to do are those things that we picked up by copying others. Paul was imitating Christ, and he wanted the Corinthians to imitate him as he was doing this. There is a false piety that strives for originality, and lands in mind-numbing conformity. There is an obedience that seeks to imitate, and the results are strikingly original. A moon facing the sun can shine its own distinct glory. A moon that wants to be a sun is going to do a very poor job of it.

But notice also that Paul moves effortlessly from "remember me in all things" to "keep the ordinances" as they had been delivered or entrusted to the Corinthians. As the subsequent discussion in this chapter shows, those ordinances had to do with things like a right relationship between the sexes in public worship and proper comportment in the Lord's Supper. Note that Paul does not assume any tension between the personal activity of remembering and imitating a person, and what some might call the impersonal activity of keeping the ordinances delivered by that person.

Paul has said that we are to imitate him as he imitates the Lord. Well, the Lord said that if we loved Him, we would keep His commandments (John 14:15). Paul looks at Jesus and imitates Him—and tells the Corinthians the very same thing. He says remember me, and keep the ordinances.

And this is why we must understand the widespread disregard for the Pauline ordinances in our day as nothing less than personal contempt for the apostle. Sometimes attempts are made to disguise that contempt, and sometimes not.

THE HEAD OF EVERY MAN

> But I would have you know, that the head of every man is Christ; and the head of the woman is the man; and the head of Christ is God. (1 Cor. 11:3)

However devoutly some people might wish it, Scripture cannot be made to fit with the dogmas of modern feminism. At some point in the attempts at reconciliation, the thought should come to mind that we ought not to waver between two opinions. If Baal is god, follow him. If Yahweh is God, follow Him.

This is one of the passages that moderns deem an embarrassment. But it says what it says regardless, and if we are Christians, our task is to understand what it is saying and to conform our lives to it.

Paul begins by saying, "I would have you know." He does not say that this is a topic that would be best left unsaid. This is something worth knowing, and it is something that we can know. He tells us that in the ordinances of the Church (which he delivered to the Corinthians, verse 2), there is an ascending hierarchy. Paul goes in the order of man and Christ, then woman and man, and then Christ and God. God is the head of Christ, Christ is the head of every man, and each man is the head of each woman.

It is worth noting here several things that it does not say. It does not say that the head of every woman is every man. The head of the woman is the man, presupposing here the marriage relationship. Neither is it talking (in this place) about the headship of Christ over the corporate Church. He does teach that in another place (Eph. 5:23), but not here.

The language is quite striking. He says that Christ is the head of *every* man. If we didn't know better, we might be tempted to say that this sounds a bit individualistic. But the Pauline doctrine is not simply that Christ is the head of the corporate bride, the Church, but that He is also the head of every man. This might be enough to make a theologian's head explode, but our task here is simply to repeat what the apostle says. If we look ahead, we see that this ascending hierarchy of headship is the foundation for the instructions that Paul is about to give—on public prayer and prophecy, on head coverings, and on appropriate demeanor in the Lord's Supper.

NO OTHER CUSTOM

> Every man praying or prophesying, having his head covered, dishonoureth his head. But every woman that prayeth or prophesieth with her head uncovered dishonoureth her head: for that is even all one as if she were shaven. For if the woman be not covered, let her also be shorn: but if it be a shame for a woman to be shorn or shaven, let her be covered. (1 Cor. 11:4–6)

This section of Corinthians has been the scene of much contention, and so we will try to work through it slowly and methodically. As for the contention—we have no other custom, and neither do the churches of God.

We will make some particular observations, but will not put them together in a larger whole until later. First, we shouldn't be precise on the head covering, but imprecise on the occasion of it. The occasion for covering or uncovering the head is during the course of prayer or prophecy on the part of that individual. While praying or prophesying, a man dishonors Christ if his head is covered. While praying or prophesying, a woman dishonors her head (her husband) if she does so while uncovered. These respective heads (Christ and husband) have just been defined in verse 3.

Secondly, this is clearly in the context of public worship. Paul is talking about the custom of the churches (v. 16). This makes it plain that the restriction the apostle places on women speaking in church later in this letter is not an absolute restriction (1 Cor. 14:34–35). She clearly may pray or prophesy in church, provided she does so in the way that the apostle stipulates will publicly honor her husband. Since prophecies have ceased, women may no longer prophesy in church for the same reason that the men cannot. Running the sail up the mast doesn't make the wind blow.

Third, a question that will arise later is one that asks whether this prohibited covering for men and mandatory covering for women is artificial (hats and veils), or natural (hair), or both. Whichever it is, we begin to see here that it has *something* to do with hair. The verb used here, *keiro*, means to cut the hair close. It is was what Paul did with regard to his Nazarite vow (Acts 18:18), and a related form applies to the shearing of sheep (Acts 8:32). So Paul is saying that if a woman goes with an uncovered head, she might as well go the entire distance and shave her head. It is commonly said (but I have not yet been able to find an ancient source for it) that the temple prostitutes at Corinth used to shave their heads. But clearly, doing something like this meant higher levels of shame.

And last, the restrictions that are placed on the time of praying or prophesying clearly have some impact on our behavior at other times. The time of praying affects the whole worship service, which affects public demeanor outside the

Church. We may limit the initial point of this instruction without trying to limit what obedience to this requirement will entail. In other words, if a woman has to have long hair by the time she prays in church, she probably ought to have that long hair a bit earlier in the service too.

THOSE PESKY HEAD COVERINGS

> For if the woman be not covered, let her also be shorn: but if it be a shame for a woman to be shorn or shaven, let her be covered. (1 Cor. 11:6)

Without coming to any final conclusions just yet, we should first consider the *if, then* possibilities. Paul says here that if the woman is not covered, she might as well be shorn. If it is a disgrace for a woman to be shorn in this way, and it is, then she should make a point of remaining covered. So, whatever "covering" means here, *not* having it is tantamount to a woman having her head buzzed.

Given the larger context, this sentence could be saying one of two things. Paul could be saying "if the woman is uncovered by a veil/shawl/hat, then she might as well have her head shaved." Or he could be saying that "if the woman has short hair, such that it does not provide a natural covering, then she might as well go all the way and have it all shaved off."

Now I am inclined to take it in the latter sense here. Saying that "a woman with *most* of her hair cut off is about the same as having *all* her hair cut off" seems to follow, in a way that saying "a woman without a hat is about the same as having all her hair cut off" does not.

This is also because to take "uncovered" as not having an artificial cover requires us to say that an uncovered woman with long hair might as well get a buzz cut. But this seems to contradict verse 15, which says that long hair is a woman's glory. As that glory, it is either an analogue to the required artificial covering, or it is that covering itself, provided by nature. But in neither case would it be tantamount to being shaved. The thing that *would* be tantamount to being shaved would be for a woman to have her hair cropped to such an extent that it did not provide her with her natural covering.

FOR A GLORY AND A COVERING

> For a man indeed ought not to cover his head, forasmuch as he is the image and glory of God: but the woman is the glory of the man. (1 Cor. 11:7)

There are several issues here that transcend the whole matter of head covering which we should address first. A man is not supposed to cover his head (again, in the context of worship) because he is the image and glory of God. This is not a requirement for men never to wear hats, even if they are exploring the Arctic. The realm of discourse here has to do with keeping the ordinances that Paul gave to the Corinthians, and all his discussion here has to do with conduct within a worship service. We do not want to absolutize this in a way that proves too much—e.g., no hats ever. I will address the question of hair/hat momentarily.

The reason a man must be uncovered in worship is that he is the image and glory of God. The reason the woman is to be covered is because she is the glory of man. Paul does not use the word image when referring to the woman, and this is because she, equally with the man, bears the image of God (Gen. 1:27).

Man is the uncovered glory of God. But when Paul says that woman is the covered glory of man, he is not trying to get the light under a bushel. His language here is redolent of the great image that Isaiah paints of a restored and forgiven Israel (and remember that for Paul, the woman represents the Church). He wants the woman covered so she can be for a glory and a covering, showing that the Lord is near. Notice where Paul gets his language of glory and covering (v. 15):

> then the LORD will create above every dwelling place of Mount Zion, and above her assemblies, a cloud and smoke by day and the shining of a flaming fire by night. For over all the glory there will be a covering. (Isa. 4:5, NKJV)

This is the shekinah glory, and the fact that some people think that Paul is in this place being insulting to women simply shows that moderns have figured out how to project their own misogyny onto him.

Now if you believe, as I do, that the primary covering reference here is to hair, and that this is the heart of the requirement, it does not follow from this that artificial coverings (veils and hats) are irrelevant to the discussion. Think of it this way. A man should have short hair (v. 14). He should have short hair, such that he is in a position to come to worship "uncovered." But what sense would it make for him to then bring a hat and wear it during worship? That would be an impudence—because he would be doing artificially (with a hat) what he is not allowed to do naturally (with hair). If he may not be covered with long hair, then how much *less* may he wear a hat in worship? With women, the logic goes the other way. If she comes to worship covered by her hair, as she ought to (v. 15), how much more may she accent that covering by artificial means? This is why the woman may wear something additional on her head, and it is also why the man may not.

The one requirement is that her covering must make the same statement that her hair was given to her to make—it must be a *glory* (v. 15). Her additional covering, if she chooses to wear one, must not be in a sad little "glory argument" with her hair. Neither may she wear her hair in a way that belies the innate glory of what God gave her.

I remember what church was like when I was a kid, especially on Easter Sunday, and especially if we sat in the balcony. Our congregation was a fair-sized lake of hats—glorious hats. This was far closer to the intent of the apostle, and kind of an affront to the grim pietists, who want the American Gothic hair to be straight and severe, the covering to be a little doily for the top, a persimmon to suck on, and for nothing to be glorious. Of course, hats can always be overdone, like aristocratic women going to the Derby at Vanity Fair, but that should be rejected too. The apostle also forbade ostentatious display (1 Tim. 2:9). A Christian woman should want to be the *glory* of her husband, not his arm candy.

SYMBOLS MATTER

> For the man is not of the woman; but the woman of the man. Neither was the man created for the woman; but the woman for the man. (1 Cor. 11:8–9)

We will return in the next verses to the application, and to the symbolism manifested in and through head coverings. Those applications are various, but the reality being applied, the symbolism being expressed, is here.

What Paul says is that we can say that the woman is of the man in a way that we cannot say in reverse. We cannot say that the man is of the woman. We can say that the woman was created for the man, and we cannot say that the man was created for the woman. We live in a day that takes high offense at things like this, and so we have to be careful. We have to take care not to make it any more offensive than it is, and we must also take care not to back away from the apostle's teaching in order to stay out of trouble. If we reject the apostle's teaching here, the only honest response would be to find a religion other than Christianity.

Paul teaches that the woman is oriented to the man differently than the man is oriented to the woman. There will be additional detail in subsequent verses, but here it says that she is "of" him, and in that same way, he is not "of" her. The man was created first, to tend the garden, and the woman was created second, to tend the gardener. She was created for him in a way that he was not created for her.

This is a creational orientation. The Fall and sin has disrupted it, and men must love their wives as Christ loved the Church in order to keep their families from being disrupted by male selfishness. But orientation toward his creational task (his garden) is not male selfishness.

This fundamental orientation is very important—so important that we need continuing and ongoing cultural reminders of it. If we ditch those reminders, we must not be surprised when we start to lose the reality as well. Symbols matter. Liturgy matters.

SIGN OF AUTHORITY

> For this cause ought the woman to have power on her head because of the angels. (1 Cor. 11:10)

The last part of this verse is obscure to us, and has generated a good bit of discussion. Because of the angels? The first question concerns whether they are celestial beings, or just ordinary messengers, or perhaps pastors (as I think they are in Revelation). I take this as a reference to celestial beings, thinking that the burden of proof should be on those who want to maintain otherwise. That is what the word usually means. The second question concerns whether the woman ought to behave in a particular way to avoid *offending* the angels, or to avoid *stumbling* them. I think there could be an element of both here, but I think it is a reference to Gen. 6:2, coupled with verse 4 of that chapter. When human societies are disordered, one of the fundamental relations that breaks down is the relationship between men and women. Christian churches should want to avoid being like those people who died in the Flood, wanting instead to be like those who were gathered into the ark.

The first part of the verse is much more straightforward. The word translated here as *woman* can also be translated as *wife*. I think it means wife here because she has to wear a particular sign of authority on her head, and to fail to do so disgraces a particular man, her husband (v. 5). She is obligated to have authority on her head. But though this has direct reference to wives, it is certainly relevant to those young women who are preparing to be wives, or those widows who have been wives. Reasoning by analogy, it is necessary for them to honor their fathers or their deceased husbands.

Put it together in this paraphrase. Because the man was not made for the woman but the woman for the man, the woman is required to have a visible indicator of his authority over her, and she must have it on her head. She must do this because the woman was created for the man, and not for the angels.

CROWN OF THE ARGUMENT

> Nevertheless neither is the man without the woman, neither the woman without the man, in the Lord. For as the woman is of the man, even so is the man also by the woman; but all things of God. (1 Cor. 11:11–12)

Paul has just finished saying that the woman was created from the man, not the other way around (v. 8). He also says that in terms of intended design, the man was not created for the woman in the same way that the woman was created for the man (v. 9). But given how such truths may be abused by sinful men (and have been), Paul makes a point of setting this earlier point in context. He doesn't want proud men thinking that they don't need women, or vice versa. In the Lord, the man is not "without" the woman, and the woman is not "without" the man.

The first woman was taken from the first man, but, Paul hastens to add, every man since Adam has been taken from the woman. In short, the sexes are entirely interdependent.

This is not a direct part of Paul's point here, but it is worth mentioning that while the first woman was taken from Adam's side, Adam himself was made from the dust of the ground—taken from the side of the earth. The word used in Genesis for the ground that Adam was taken from is *adamah*, which is adam with a feminine ending. No one has an autonomous starting point. We should sum it up the way Paul does, which is by saying that all things are of God (v. 12).

It is also important to note that this discussion of the interdependency of the sexes is not a shift in topic. Paul is still talking about head coverings—this is a long and sustained narrative about head coverings. He is building toward the climax of his argument, which is that the created order testifies to the reality of the interdependent relationship of the sexes. We will next see how the topics of hair and headship are the crown of his argument.

WHAT NATURE TEACHES

> Judge in yourselves: is it comely that a woman pray unto God uncovered? Doth not even nature itself teach you, that, if a man have long hair, it is a shame unto him? But if a woman have long hair, it is a glory to her: for her hair is given her for a covering. But if any

man seem to be contentious, we have no such custom, neither the churches of God. (1 Cor. 11:13–16)

So we now come to what I believe is the nub of Paul's argument. He has grounded his argument in the way the world was created—so I do not think we can legitimately evade his requirement by appeal to Greco/Roman customs. What Paul is teaching in 1 Corinthians is something that "nature itself" also teaches. That doctrine is that women should have a covering on their heads when they pray in public, and that men should not. This is natural theology, and it is reinforced by special revelation.

My reading of this is that a woman's long hair is given her "for a covering" (v. 15). I do not take it as her long hair is given her "for an illustration of how an additional covering is necessary." So the lesson is brought to us by nature, and the provision for Paul's requirement is given to us by nature as well.

But what nature teaches here is nevertheless relevant to man-made coverings. If a man has short hair and prays in church with a baseball cap on, he is violating the intent of this passage—even though he has short hair. But if a woman has long hair and wears an additional covering (a veil, covering, or hat), she is accentuating the import of the passage.

Those who do not see this passage as requiring man-made coverings may not therefore dismiss what the passage is actually requiring. Women who do not wear an artificial covering must make a point of making sure that their hair—given them for a covering—actually serves as one. It is not possible to argue that because long hair is given for a covering, this means that long hair is not necessary.

And this leads to the final question. What does "long" mean here? How long before it is a shame to a man? How long before it is a glory to a woman? There are two aspects to this answer. Note that the Bible does not give us quantitative measurements—"over twelve inches," say. This means that long and short should be defined from the context of the passage, and there are two aspects we should think about. First, the long and short are used as a comparison between men and women. A woman's hair should be long relative to the man's, and in particular, relative to her husband's. When I was a boy, my father had short hair (crew cut) and my mother had long hair (shoulder length). When our kids were little, I had short hair (shoulder length) and Nancy had long hair (down to her waist). This rule of thumb is obviously not completely elastic—say if a man had hair four and a half feet long, we should notice the problem even if his wife had hair six inches longer than that.

The second aspect of this is that hair is given "for a covering." A man should not have enough hair to wear it that way, and a woman should. This would prevent the opposite "technical solution" of a man with a buzz cut and a woman with hair that is one inch long. Hair is given to the woman for a glory and a covering—and should be received as such.

One last thing, which should be obvious, but I will say it anyway. We are not talking about the exceptional situations—women who lose their hair during chemo, for example.

DECORUM AND DECENCY

> Now in this that I declare unto you I praise you not, that ye come together not for the better, but for the worse. (1 Cor. 11:17)

Paul here returns to the subject of the Lord's Supper, which I don't believe he ever entirely left. He covered the Lord's Table in the first part of chapter 10, which then blended readily into his discussion of pagan sacrifices. With chapter 11, he moved into his discussion of sexual orderliness, which is what the head coverings were all about. And here, in verse 17, he comes back to how the Corinthians are coming together in "communion." I see him bringing his thought full circle—he is not jumping randomly from one topic to another. Our sacrifice of praise led to a discussion of the meat the pagans sacrificed to idols, which led to a discussion of sexual propriety in worship. This brings him back to the point he was driving to all along—the disorderliness of their worship.

Christian worship can do more harm than good. We can be worse off after a service than when we went in. Grace is not imparted automatically. Coming to the Lord's Table can leave us worse off than if we had not come. This is because it is a covenant meal, not a magic meal. Covenants have terms. They can be honored or broken. The way this covenant is honored is by means of faith alone, and if we are coming to worship in the only kind of faith that God gives, which is living faith, then we will not be doing destructive things to our neighbor, and to our own souls because of that.

But when the relationships between husbands and wives in a church are disordered, that means that when they come together the disorder will be apparent. That obvious disorder will be used either as an excuse for immorality, or as an opportunity for it. When men are in conflict with one another, the top three reasons are women, money, and glory. In this stretch of his letter, Paul is treating all three.

SCHISM AND HERESY

> For first of all, when ye come together in the church, I hear that there be divisions among you; and I partly believe it. For there must be also heresies among you, that they which are approved may be made manifest among you. (1 Cor. 11:18–19)

Paul has already told us that Christian worship might be making things worse. He now gets to the reason. When the congregation gathers together as one, it becomes apparent that they are *not* one. There are divisions (schisms) among them, and Paul says that he partly believes it. This means that he thinks things are bad, but probably not quite as bad as he has heard. He partly believes it. He then says that it is necessary that there be heresies among them, in order to reveal who the good guys are.

This last comment—"who the good guys are"—can be read straight, or as a sarcastic shot at the faction leaders. In the former reading, the development of factions reveals to us which Christians are avoiding the sins of factionalism. In the latter reading, the development of factions is done so that the factionalists can demonstrate to everyone how wonderful—how "approved"—they must be. When you form the factional club yourself, the entry requirements can always be met.

The word heresy came later to be identified with foundational doctrinal error, but here it probably means that sectarian spirit that—in order to maintain the schism—comes up with weird doctrines in order to justify the split retroactively. Understood this way, heresy in the latter sense grows out of schism, and the need to be different. Jeroboam did not divide Israel for the sake of the golden calves at Dan and at Beersheba, but the idea occurred to him almost right away as a way of maintaining his new territory.

Paul views this as a matter of necessity. For we live in a fallen world, and it "must be" that this will happen. I have seen it happen over and over and over again. Whenever a congregation grows to a particular size, someone will develop an itch to distinguish himself, and he will have to cook up a reason (Acts 20:30). Sometimes an actual reason does exist, but whether a good reason is available or not, he will always be up to the challenge.

EXTRA PORTIONS AT THE LORD'S TABLE

> When ye come together therefore into one place, this is not to eat the Lord's supper. For in eating every one taketh before other his own supper: and one is hungry, and another is drunken. What? have ye not houses to eat and to drink in? or despise ye the church of God, and shame them that have not? What shall I say to you? shall I praise you in this? I praise you not. (1 Cor. 11:20–22)

Paul—in a typical move—says that when the Corinthians gather to eat the Lord's Supper, they are not gathering to eat the Lord's Supper. The evidence for this that Paul cites is that one person rushes ahead to eat his own food, another person is left out, and somebody else gets drunk. Clearly this is happening at Corinth because the Lord's Supper was occurring in the context of a love feast. There was enough food there for people to be greedy with it. If you want to eat your own food, Paul says, then why don't you eat and drink in your own homes? When you bring the disparities that exist between rich and poor into the Lord's Supper, you are undoing the purpose of the Supper.

Benjamin got a much bigger portion than his brothers because Joseph was showing him favor. Joseph gave him five times as much (Gen. 43:34). Saul, a son of Benjamin, got a choice portion when he sat down at the banquet because Samuel was showing him favor (1 Sam. 9:24). If we were to allow the rich man in our assembly—the big tither—to have a much bigger portion, our observance of the Supper would be declaring a falsehood. Allowing something like that to occur in the Supper is to introduce distinctions at the Supper that the Supper was designed to undo.

When we allow this kind of income discrepancy to become manifest in the Supper, we are doing sacramentally what James prohibits in the seating arrangements (Jas. 2:3). We are making distinctions that have no place in our midst. When we behave in a way that shames those without, we are despising the Church of God. We cannot despise the Church of God without also despising the Table in the midst of the Church of God. And if we despise the Table while we are sitting around it, we are not really observing the Lord's Supper. It is not the Lord's Supper that we are partaking of—even though it is the Lord's Supper we are despising.

THE LORD AND THE LORD'S SUPPER WERE BOTH HANDED OVER

> For I have received of the Lord that which also I delivered unto you, That the Lord Jesus the same night in which he was betrayed took bread (1 Cor. 11:23)

In the verses to follow, we will discuss the administration of the Lord's Supper itself. Here we should begin by noting where Paul got what he is about to pass on to the Corinthians. Paul was not present when the Lord instituted the Supper, and yet he says here that he received what he is about to say from the Lord. He received it from the Lord directly—he says "I received it."

When he received it, he handed over, delivered what he had received. The word used for delivered here is *paradidomi*. This is striking because it is the same word that he uses in the very next phrase when he describes how Jesus was betrayed, or handed over.

Now this means that when the Lord was getting the apostle Paul "up to speed"—for he was like one untimely born (1 Cor. 15:8)—one of the topics the Lord covered with Paul was the subject of the Lord's Supper. Paul makes a point of insisting that he did not get the message he preached from the other apostles (Gal. 1:15–17). That means that the resurrected and ascended Lord included this subject on the syllabus He was covering with Paul. Jesus, teaching Paul, remembered what He had done for His disciples the night He was betrayed. And Paul handed this remembrance over to the Corinthians, just as Judas had handed Jesus over to the chief priests.

TAKE AND EAT

> And when he had given thanks, he brake it, and said, Take, eat: this is my body, which is broken for you: this do in remembrance of me. (1 Cor. 11:24)

This is Paul's recounting of how the Lord instituted the Supper, an account that he had received from the Lord Himself (v. 23). The first thing to note is that Jesus gave thanks, and then broke the bread. He knew what the import of this breaking was, because He mentions that in the next breath. He said that the broken bread was His broken body, and when He broke the bread as an enactment of this, He prefaced it by giving thanks over the breaking of His own body.

Second, He said, "take" and "eat." He didn't say "take and dispute" or "take and worship." The actions involved are *taking, eating,* and *remembering.*

Third, there is some discussion over the meaning of word translated "remembrance" here, some taking it as memorial, and others as remembrance. Memorial would be more expansive, meaning that God will remember in our observance, just as He remembers with the appearance of the rainbow. But in either case, we are to remember, we are to recall.

PROCLAIMING BY REMEMBRANCE

> After the same manner also he took the cup, when he had supped, saying, This cup is the new testament in my blood: this do ye, as oft as ye drink it, in

> remembrance of me. For as often as ye eat this bread, and drink this cup, ye do shew the Lord's death till he come. (1 Cor. 11:25–26)

Jesus picked up the cup in the "same manner" as He had done with the loaf. We have two elements, but one sacrament. He said something through the bread, and then He said the same thing again through the wine. The bread and the wine are therefore synonyms—they both refer to Christ sacrificed. The bread represents His body, and the wine represents the life of His body.

The cup is His blood, and the cup is also the new testament. This means that His blood is the new testament—Jesus makes this explicit by saying "new testament in my blood." As often as we drink the wine, we are to do so as a remembrance of Christ. He then ties it up together again by saying that we are doing the same thing whenever we eat the bread or drink the cup—we are showing, displaying, the Lord's death until He comes again. The word rendered as "show" is *katangello,* and can be translated as "announce" or "proclaim." This helps us define what we are doing in the remembrance. We remember the Lord in such a way as to proclaim Him to those who are outside the covenant.

UP AND DOWN THE PEW

> Wherefore whosoever shall eat this bread, and drink this cup of the Lord, unworthily, shall be guilty of the body and blood of the Lord. But let a man examine himself, and so let him eat of that bread, and drink of

that cup. For he that eateth and drinketh unworthily, eateth and drinketh damnation to himself, not discerning the Lord's body. (1 Cor. 11:27–29)

Before discussing the theology of the sin committed here, we need to first identify what sin it is. The sin is found and named at the end of verse 29—it is the sin of "not discerning the Lord's body." The first and fundamental error is that of looking for the Lord's body in the bread and in the cup, instead of in the place where we truly neglect the Lord's body, which is up and down the pew we are sitting in. In the previous chapter, we are told that the cup and the bread are a *koinonia*, a partaking, a fellowship in the blood and body of Christ (1 Cor. 10:16). In the next verse, we are told that we, being many, are one bread and one body, and we are that because of our mutual partaking (1 Cor. 10:17).

To exclude children from the Supper, therefore, because they are not up the challenge of Eucharistic metaphysics with the bread and the wine placed under a theological microscope is to miss the point in a jaw-dropping way. Those who are bread should get bread, and those who exclude those little ones for not "discerning" the Lord's body are themselves not discerning the Lord's body. A man who says that somebody else can't come because he is not capable of examining himself adequately is not examining himself. Examine yourself, the apostle says. Are you placing any unbiblical and unnecessary barriers between you and any other member of Christ's body? That was the problem at Corinth, and it is still a problem.

The other important issue that this passage raises is the question of what is meant by unworthy eating and drinking. This is one of the distinctions that separates the Reformed understanding of the Supper from the Lutheran. The Reformed affirm that there is a *manducatio indigna*, an unworthy eating, but deny that there is a *manducatio indignorum*, an eating (of Christ) by the unworthy. At issue is different views of the "real presence" in the bread and wine. What Paul says the unworthy receiver is eating and drinking is damnation (v. 29). On one view, he is partaking of damnation because he is eating and drinking an undiscerned Christ (in the bread and wine). But the view I am advancing says that he is damned because he is eating and drinking *with* an undiscerned Christ (the body of Christ surrounding him). Because of this, he is guilty of the body and blood of the Lord. Our natural tendency is to locate the sacrilege in the treatment of the elements, rather than where Paul places it, in our treatment of our brothers and sisters. Do you discern the body in the body? *That's* the question.

This includes, incidentally, our treatment of our brothers and sisters who differ with us on what is entailed in the Lord's Supper. Suppose a man does everything "wrong" from my perspective. He uses grape juice, he observes it quarterly, and he is a mere memorialist . . . and he loves everybody in the sanctuary with a true heart. He is a true partaker, while a more orthodox man who approaches it unworthily drinks damnation wine, drinks it weekly, and despises the saints. He is guilty of the Lord's body and blood.

Anybody who forgets that the Supper is a covenantal meal has forgotten that it is a place of winnowing.

QUICK TO BE CORRECTED

> For this cause many are weak and sickly among you, and many sleep. For if we would judge ourselves, we should not be judged. But when we are judged, we are chastened of the Lord, that we should not be condemned with the world. (1 Cor. 11:30–32)

So the Lord's Supper is a place for winnowing. It is not a vending machine, full of automatic blessings, but rather a covenantal meal, and we are communing with the Lord of that meal (and His people) in love and respect, or we are not doing so. If we are not, then the dislocations in our relationships will also show up in our relationship to the meal. The meal embodies what should be going on, as well as embodying what is going on.

God would not have to administer the correction if we were quicker to administer it to ourselves. God doesn't spank His children for the sake of spanking them, but rather so that they will learn something about themselves. But if they are quick to learn it themselves, if in this area we run ahead of the Lord, we are doing well. God does not have to bring external chastisement if we bring it internally first.

But if we drag our feet, and the Lord does have to bring external chastisement, He is doing it because He loves us. The point of His discipline is so that we not be condemned along with the world.

This means that we have two divisions. The first is between the world and the saints. The world is condemned already, and the people of God are not. But within the congregation, we find another division. We have saints who have to learn things the hard way and saints who are eager to receive correction from the Spirit. This latter group is not made up of the morbidly introspective, incidentally, who confess any sin but the one they are committing. It is made up of those who are quick to hear what the Spirit is saying to them. If He admonishes them for something, it is for them as oil on the head (Ps. 141:5).

COMMUNION AND LOVE FEAST

> Wherefore, my brethren, when ye come together to eat, tarry one for another. And if any man hunger, let him eat at home; that ye come not together unto condemnation. And the rest will I set in order when I come. (1 Cor. 11:33–34)

In the early church, the Lord's Supper was celebrated in the context of a communal meal—a love feast. This explains how it was possible for someone to get drunk at one, or to hog some of the food. It was a potluck that was conjoined to the Eucharistic celebration. It also provides us with a good example of how we are not necessarily called to try to duplicate the practices of the early church. This is what they did, but Paul was kind of nervous about it, and in this place was riding the brake a little bit.

When it is time to eat, he urged them to wait on one another. And if someone is hungry in a physical sense, Paul said that he should take care of that at home. If you come hungry, you will be tempted to use the Supper as a time for satisfying physical appetite, and that is not what it is for.

If you approach it that way, your gathering, which ought to be for blessing, will actually be for condemnation. Stay out of trouble, Paul says, and he will fix things even more when he comes.

CHAPTER 12

LED AND MISLED

> Now concerning spiritual gifts, brethren, I would not have you ignorant. Ye know that ye were Gentiles, carried away unto these dumb idols, even as ye were led. Wherefore I give you to understand, that no man speaking by the Spirit of God calleth Jesus accursed: and that no man can say that Jesus is the Lord, but by the Holy Ghost. (1 Cor. 12:1–3)

Paul then turns decidedly to a new topic, which is the subject of spiritual gifts. He announces the topic, and says that he wants to bring it up because he doesn't want the Corinthian Christians to be ignorant of it. He wants to talk about what it means to be *led* by the Spirit in the matter of gifts, and the very first thing he introduces is the possibility of being *misled*.

He appears to be changing the subject, but that is not what he is doing at all. He reminds them of what it was like when they were Gentiles, before they had been ushered into the new Israel. He does not say that they used to "worship idols." He says that they were "carried away" to dumb idols, "even as ye were led." They were led somewhere, they were carried somewhere, and this had to have been done *by something*. In other words, spiritual forces were operative in their lives before they were converted, and there is no reason to believe that these evil spiritual forces have gone away. This means that within the context of the Christian Church, it is still necessary to be on guard against false and lying spirits. Just as in the past, they would lead their captives to dumb idols, so now they might lead a professing Christian to say something outrageous to a dumb idol that has been set up in the sanctuary.

Paul then gives two tests, one negative and one positive. If a spirit calls Jesus "accursed," then it is not by the Spirit of God. And conversely, if someone in the spirit confesses that Jesus is Lord, then it is by the Holy Spirit. It is easy to see how someone in the grip of a blasphemous spirit might take the truth that Jesus became a curse for us on the tree (Gal. 3:13), and bend it slightly in order to take spiritual glee in *italicizing* the word "curse." But confessing the lordship of Jesus is not something they can bring themselves to do.

So Paul starts his instruction on spiritual gifts by warning the Corinthians of the great danger that a thoughtless approach to it creates.

EXPLORING DIVERSITY

> Now there are diversities of gifts, but the same Spirit. And there are differences of administrations, but the same Lord. And there are diversities of operations, but it is the same God which worketh all in all. (1 Cor. 12:4–6)

We need to begin our discussion of the spiritual gifts with a recognition that the whole thing is an exercise in Trinitarian theology. There is one purpose that runs throughout the manifestation of all true gifts—because there is one God. There are many different displays of God's power because there is first the Spirit (v. 4), then the Lord (v. 5), and then God (v. 6).

So the differences between "diversities of gifts" or "differences of administrations," or the "diversities of operations" are not themselves unworthy of God. God is not an infinite and undefined extension of Newtonian space. God is triune, and exuberantly creative. We must not disparage the manifestation of this gift here and a completely different gift over there, any more than we would slight the fact that the same God created the sea lion and the little yellow canary. That is how our God is. This is how the problem of the one and the many resolves—it resolves in the one God, who is Spirit, Lord, and God. This one God has one purpose and many tools.

So diversity is not unworthy of Him. We saw in the first verses of this chapter that there are spurious gifts, displays of spirituality that lead into idolatry. But the mere fact of differences cannot be used as an argument against the legitimacy of a gift. We should expect differences in our gifts.

GIFTS THAT PROFIT

> But the manifestation of the Spirit is given to every man to profit withal. (1 Cor. 12:7).

Let's begin our discussion of this passage by citing a more contemporary translation. "To each is given the manifestation of the Spirit for the common good" (1 Cor. 12:7, ESV). We have many different gifts, with many manifestations, but there is one common theme. All of these things are given by God (the Spirit) in order to establish the common good, or common advantage. To anticipate a metaphor that is coming up, there is one body, with one interest—that of staying alive—and the different gifts are like different organs or members of that body. The liver does one thing, for the common good, while the kidneys do something completely different, also for the same common good.

This means that we cannot dismiss the liver because it is not acting like the stomach or the kidneys. But we can object if the liver is acting like a diseased liver, or perhaps like a rock or a stone. The liver doesn't act like the stomach, but a stone doesn't act like the stomach either. Gifts are tested, not by whether they match a different gift or not, but by whether or not they benefit the common good. Genuine gifts bring that profit; spurious gifts do not.

BEACH BOYS GLOSSOLALIA

> For to one is given by the Spirit the word of wisdom; to another the word of knowledge by the same Spirit; To another faith by the same Spirit; to another the gifts of healing by the same Spirit; To another the working of miracles; to another prophecy; to another discerning of spirits; to another divers kinds of tongues; to another the interpretation of tongues: But all these worketh that one and the selfsame Spirit, dividing to every man severally as he will. (1 Cor. 12:8–11)

Paul's point here in this passage is to point out the fact that multiple workings are all proceeding from one source, which means that these multiple gifts are all meant to work toward one unified purpose or end. He does this by saying the Spirit does x, the *same* Spirit does y, and the *same* Spirit does z.

The first gift mentioned is the word of wisdom (v. 8), and the second is the word of knowledge (v. 8). A third gift is that of faith (v. 9), and a fourth is the gift of healing (v. 9). Another man can work miracles (v. 10), yet another can prophesy (v. 10), and another can discern spirits (v. 10). Someone else has the gift of various languages (v. 10), and someone else can interpret (v. 10). But the one source of the diverse gifts is the one Spirit, who exercises His sovereignty by dispensing these gifts as He sees fit.

We do not know precisely what the gifts of wisdom and knowledge were, but judging from the face value of the words, it would be something like a timely statement of what the people should *do* (wisdom) and what the people should *know* (knowledge). The gift of faith appears to be the gift of remarkable faith, out of the ordinary faith—because every Christian has faith. It would be the gift of believing for particular things, as George Mueller did.

The gift of healing is possessed by someone who can heal someone else, with power draining from him as it happens—as when the woman with the hemorrhaging touched the Lord and was healed. The *gift* of healing should be distinguished from *answered prayer* healing. The gift of healing is not possessed by anyone today, and neither is the gift of miracles (2 Cor. 12:12). Prophecy proper is not possessed by anyone either, although elements of the prophetic office are still present in preaching. We do not have anyone today who can write new Scripture. But we *do* have men who can speak in the name of the Lord.

A person who can discern spirits would be necessary in a service when people were speaking prophetically in a service under the influence of a spirit—Paul himself gave guidance on discerning spirits at the beginning of this chapter (v. 3). My understanding is that the gift of languages and interpretation together should be considered the equivalent to prophecy, which means that this gift is no longer extant.

Now some will no doubt object to all the "cessationism," and say that they themselves have spoken in tongues or have been in services where that has happened. What about that? It reminds me of Mark Twain's response when asked if he believed in infant baptism. "Believe in it? I have seen it *done*!" My understanding of the gift of tongues is that it is the gift of *languages*—with a vocabulary, grammar, syntax, meaning, the whole deal. We are too easily impressed with or persuaded by what could be called Beach Boys glossolalia—ba ba ba ba ba *ran*.

Having offended one half of the Church, let me proceed to offend the other. But I *mean* well.

The fact that I believe that this kind of gifted authority was vested in, or was resident in, particular saints prior to the close of the canon, and is not operative today in the same way, does *not* mean that I believe the Holy Spirit died, or that God does not answer prayers, or that He is not actively at work in the world in visible and remarkable ways. I believe that the gift of miracle-working has ceased, not that miracles have ceased. I believe that the gift of healing has ceased, not that healing has ceased. And so on. What I believe has been taken out of the picture is any genuine spiritual gift that would provide anyone with a cogent scriptural argument that would require us to believe that person to be an apostle.

There will be more on this subject as we proceed through this portion of this epistle.

ONE BODY, MANY MEMBERS

> For as the body is one, and hath many members, and all the members of that one body, being many, are one body: so also is Christ. For by one Spirit are we

> all baptized into one body, whether we be Jews or Gentiles, whether we be bond or free; and have been all made to drink into one Spirit. For the body is not one member, but many. (1 Cor. 12:12–14)

Paul then comes to introduce his central illustration for the use of spiritual gifts, which is the illustration of one body with many different organs. He says, first, the body is one, but the one body has many members. He then comes from the opposite direction, and says that there are many members, but they are all part of one body. This is the way Christ is, because this is the way the body of Christ is. Christ has one body—His Church—and this one body has many different members.

We are members of this body by virtue of the baptism of the Spirit, which is described as the baptism of one Spirit. Whether you are Jew or Gentile, slave or free, tall or short, you were baptized into one body by the same Spirit who baptized all the other members into that same body. Not only were we all baptized by one Spirit, he adds that we all drank from that same one Spirit.

The body therefore has different organs, different members, and as Paul puts it here, there are *many* different members. This is contrasted to the negative, where Paul says that while we are all one body, we are not all one member.

MOST OF WHAT WE DO WE MOSTLY CAN'T DO

> If the foot shall say, Because I am not the hand, I am not of the body; is it therefore not of the body? And if the ear shall say, Because I am not the eye, I am

> not of the body; is it therefore not of the body? If the whole body were an eye, where were the hearing? If the whole were hearing, where were the smelling? (1 Cor. 12:15–17)

Before going on to apply the illustration of the human body to spiritual gifts, it is important for us to take in the various points presented by the illustration. The first point is that unity is unavoidable (v. 15). The foot cannot say that being not-a-hand means that the foot is outside the body. Regardless of what the foot says about it, it is in the same body with the hand—despite the fact that they are not at all alike. Their functions are dissimilar, but they are parts of the same body nonetheless. Paul makes the same point over again with the ear and the eye (v. 16). If the ear notices that it is not an eye, and that premise may be true enough, but the conclusion that it is not "of the body" does not follow. It remains in the same body together with the eye. Paul's second point is that the hidden logic here destroys the very idea of a body. If the whole body were an eye, that whole body would be deaf. If the whole body were an ear, then there would be no way to smell.

This is another way of saying that your elbows, both of them, are blind. Your feet are deaf. The back of your neck is dumb.

But when you see, your eyes fill your whole body with light. Your elbows don't feel blind. You don't *feel* like only one percent of your body sees. You see. Each part performs its function on behalf of all the others, and all the others rely on it to perform that function. Moreover, each blind part quits trying to see and focuses on doing what it was designed to do—and which the eyes cannot do. The eyes cannot carry oxygen to the remote parts of the body, so that must be done for them.

AS IT HAS PLEASED HIM

> But now hath God set the members every one of them in the body, as it hath pleased him. (1 Cor. 12:18)

In the lines preceding this, Paul has been using the illustration of the human body. The eye cannot hear, the ear cannot see, and so forth. And just after this, in verse 21, he returns to the illustration again in order to reinforce the point. In the two verses just after this one, he applies the concept to spiritual gifts.

Before getting to that point, however, the center of this verse must be pressed home. The body of Christ has many different members in it, and each one of them is where it is because God has placed it there. "God set the members." This point is reinforced with Paul's follow up phrase—"as it hath pleased him."

Some gifts are up front, as the eyes are. Other gifts are down inside, completely out of sight, like the gifts that the liver has. God has positioned everyone in exactly the right place. God is *pleased* with that positioning.

Of course in a world where sin has an impact, we do want to learn to do better. But we can never accomplish this by envying the position of another. In other words, an eye should want to see better, and not to hear at all. An ear should want to hear better, and not to smell at all. Each of us should want to be just where God designed us to be, doing a better job in that place.

PRIDE IN THE BODY

> And if they were all one member, where were the body? But now are they many members, yet but one body. And the eye cannot say unto the hand, I have no need of thee: nor again the head to the feet, I have no need of you. (1 Cor. 12:19–21)

Paul has been arguing for the interdependence of the various parts of the body. In the previous illustration, he talks about a member exiling himself from the body simply because he was not another member. The foot cannot separate itself from the body because it is not a hand. The ear cannot separate itself because it is not an eye. This separation might occur because a member thinks that it is not worthy enough to be with the others.

But in this next round of comparisons, Paul has parts of the body becoming proud. He has established the principle that one body is made up of many members. And in the false understanding of this, he now rejects the pride that makes one part say to another member that the *other* member is unnecessary. The eye cannot say to the hand that the hand is not needed. The head cannot say that to the foot.

COVERED UP IN HONOR

> Nay, much more those members of the body, which seem to be more feeble, are necessary: And those

> members of the body, which we think to be less honourable, upon these we bestow more abundant honour; and our uncomely parts have more abundant comeliness. (1 Cor. 12:22–23)

Paul is willing to push the analogy pretty far. He has been arguing that the eye needs the ear, and vice versa, but he now moves on to the matter of honor—and does so in order to reverse the common expectation. He first says that parts of the body that seem to be "more feeble" are every bit as necessary as parts of the body which seem naturally honorable. He says that we go out of our way to clothe the less honorable parts of our body with beautiful fabric, but we don't do anything like that to the forehead. Paul here is arguing from more than simple biological fact—he is arguing from the universal human custom of clothing and "covering for" the less honorable parts.

But do not assume that if one part of the body is always kept away from the microphone that this represents contempt. It is actually the way we cover for one another in love. Some parts of the body can be exposed, and others cannot be, but all parts of the body should be working together in love.

COMPENSATORY HONOR

> For our comely parts have no need: but God hath tempered the body together, having given more abundant honour to that part which lacked: That there should be no schism in the body; but that the members should have the same care one for another. (1 Cor. 12:24–25)

So the body is naturally solicitous for the parts of the body that have less honor. There is a natural modesty we have, given by God, which causes us to compensate. The "comely parts" need no additional honor through clothing or jewelry, but other parts do. This giving of additional care to certain parts of the body is described as God "tempering the body together."

When we do this, we are avoiding schism, he says, and the goal is for the different members of the body to have what he calls the "same care" for one another. And what he has described is a paradox. We provide one another with the same care by making sure we provide one another with different care. To recognize that some parts are less presentable enables you to clothe the congregation in such a way that the whole congregation is presentable. If you treat everyone exactly the same out of a false idea of "equality," you are going to make the God-given inequalities worse. You want the whole thing to even out—and so some parts of the body are clothed and some parts are not.

THE SAME NERVOUS SYSTEM

> And whether one member suffer, all the members suffer with it; or one member be honoured, all the members rejoice with it. Now ye are the body of Christ, and members in particular. (1 Cor. 12:26–27)

Not only do we adjust for one another, so that the more presentable parts of the body are presented and the less presentable parts are covered, but we also share the same spiritual nervous system. If one member of the body is in pain, then the entire body experiences the pain. If one part is glorified, then the entire body rejoices.

So Paul then gathers up all the illustrations from the body he has been using and says that the Corinthians together are the body of Christ, and he says that each one of them is a particular member. They are therefore interconnected, and should function with that interconnectedness in the way he has been describing.

THE IT GUY

> And God hath set some in the church, first apostles, secondarily prophets, thirdly teachers, after that miracles, then gifts of healings, helps, governments, diversities of tongues. (1 Cor. 12:28)

When Paul gives a list of spiritual gifts, as he does here, it is not meant to be a comprehensive or exhaustive list. Rather, such lists need to be understood as representative samples of the gifts that are operative within the body. We can tell this from the fact that he gives such lists in different places, and the lists of gifts are not identical. For example, we have the listing here, but another one in Romans:

> Having then gifts differing according to the grace that is given to us, whether prophecy, let us prophesy according to the proportion of faith; Or ministry, let us wait on our ministering: or he that teacheth, on teaching; Or he that exhorteth, on exhortation: he that giveth, let him do it with simplicity; he that ruleth, with diligence; he that sheweth mercy, with cheerfulness. (Rom. 12:6–8)

In Ephesians, he gives us a much shorter list. "And he gave some, apostles; and some, prophets; and some, evangelists; and some, pastors and teachers" (Eph. 4:11).

There are different approaches to this. Some might want to simply combine the lists, remove the redundancies, and say that "those" are the gifts, period. Another approach, one I am inclined to, says that we need to accept the functioning of all listed gifts within biblical parameters, but we may also be open to the possibility of other gifts not expressly mentioned in these lists. One example might be that of a gifted computer tech guy on the church staff. If we were pressed to use a biblical name for him, we could just call him the exorcist.

DO ALL SPEAK IN TONGUES?

> Are all apostles? are all prophets? are all teachers? are all workers of miracles? Have all the gifts of healing? do all speak with tongues? do all interpret? (1 Cor. 12:29–30)

Paul is bringing his extended analogy in for a landing. He has been comparing the body of Christ to a physical body, and arguing that different individuals in the body are like different organs of the body—all having different functions, but with the well-being and health of the one body as their common goal and purpose.

He concludes with a series of rhetorical questions. A rhetorical question is one that is asked without expecting an explicit answer . . . because the answer is implied and obvious. The answer to all the questions here is obviously *no*. Is everyone supposed to be an apostle? *No.* Should everyone be a prophet? *No.* Is everyone supposed to be a teacher? *No.* Does everyone have the power to work miracles? *No.* Can everyone exercise the gift of healing? *No.* Should everyone speak in tongues? *No.* Should everyone interpret tongues? *No.*

This is the capstone of Paul's argument about body life, and we could move on, but there is one item of continuing interest here. Not a few modern Christians maintain that everyone is supposed to speak in tongues, even though Paul says that this was not the case, even when the gift of tongues was extant.

SPIRITUAL GIFTS AND UNSPIRITUAL MEN

> But covet earnestly the best gifts: and yet shew I unto you a more excellent way. (1 Cor. 12:31)

Paul is now moving into his very famous chapter on love, and the last verse of chapter 12 is actually the first verse of chapter 13.

In order to understand his argument here, and the juxtaposition he sets up, we have to understand that gifts of the Spirit are good, if they are used rightly, and the fruit of the Spirit is good, by definition. If the Holy Spirit has given someone the gift of teaching, he has that gift on days he is walking with God and on days when he is not. When someone is exhibiting the fruit of the Spirit, by definition he is doing right. Teaching, administration, encouragement, etc. can all happen when the practitioner is not right with God. But love, joy, and peace cannot.

In this verse, Paul urges the Corinthians to desire the "best gifts," which is referring to the gifts he has been discussing in the previous chapter. But he then relativizes that whole discussion by introducing them to a "more excellent way."

Remember that Paul began this letter by saying that the Corinthians had all the spiritual gifts; they were not lacking in any (1 Cor. 1:7). At the same time, he could not address them as spiritual men, but rather as carnal, as babes in Christ (1 Cor. 3:1). Put another way, spiritual gifts may be given to unspiritual men—there is tension in that, but no logical contradiction. It is not right, but it is not a round square either. But spiritual fruit cannot be given to men without making them spiritual men.

And so it is a more excellent way. Jesus taught us that love would be the "tell," the way nonbelievers would be able to see that we do in fact belong to Christ (John 13:35).

CHAPTER 13

NEVER IN SHADOW

Though I speak with the tongues of men and of angels, and have not charity, I am become as sounding brass, or a tinkling cymbal. And though I have the gift of prophecy, and understand all mysteries, and all knowledge; and though I have all faith, so that I could remove mountains, and have not charity, I am nothing. And though I bestow all my goods to feed the poor, and though I give my body to be burned, and have not charity, it profiteth me nothing. (1 Cor. 13:1–3)

Paul has promised to show us a more excellent way, which is the way of love, and he begins by contrasting it with some of its more common substitutes. Those substitutes we might describe as rhetoric, genuine knowledge, powerful faith, mercy work, and martyrdom.

Since Paul is clearly not against those things in themselves, then the task is clearly to make sure that they are done, when they are done, with the right motives and in the right way. The right motives and the right way is necessarily the way of charity. If charity is not involved, then the rhetoric of angels is tantamount to becoming an irritating percussion instrument. If charity is not the driving force, then the ability to explain everything and move anything is coming from a puff of nothing. And in a move that is surprising to some, Paul is not here contrasting words with deeds. He is contrasting loveless words and deeds with love-driven words and deeds. His next example concerns the person who, apart from love, gives all his possessions to the poor—as Jesus told the rich, young ruler to do. There is no profit; it profits him nothing. Such a man loses all his possessions and his treasure in Heaven. The same thing goes for the martyr who dies in the flames—it is possible to get there from the wrong motives.

Such a grim and cynical beginning to this chapter might cause some to despair. If this is the case, then who can be saved? If this is the case, then how can we ever know if we are following Christ rightly? The following verses show us that love is always out in the sunlight, and never in the shadow. Love is not hiding in the gray areas. Love is pretty obvious, as we will soon see.

LOVE IS NOT FURTIVE

> Charity suffereth long, and is kind; charity envieth not; charity vaunteth not itself, is not puffed up, (1 Cor. 13:4)

We have come to a famous and very exalted passage, the apostle Paul's paean to love. Given the nature of the case, and the nature of our particular shortfalls, it would be a shame to rush through it.

A common preacher's trick is to have everyone substitute their own name for the word love here, and then to ask searchingly how everyone measures up. The answer of course is no one, and we are all suitably chastened and abashed, and crawl home like a dog that's been beat too much. But that response is not fitting, not even on its own terms. The passage does not end with "Charity is furtive, and guilty; charity does not know where to look."

We are Christians, and we follow Christ, and He is the one who has liberated us. So we should begin by substituting the name of the Lord Jesus here. It fits perfectly, and it is consistent with good news. Because *He* is like this, we are not consumed.

Love is longsuffering. It does not rush to judgment as soon as it sees the logical conclusion. Love is therefore frequently imposed upon. Love gives it another go. Love appears to have people taking advantage.

Love is kind. Kindness is thoughtful, tender. Kindness is considerate. Kindness anticipates.

Love is free of the sidelong glance. Love is not envious, which means that love knows how to rejoice when God's kindness and blessing is visited upon another. Love rejoices in inequality. Love throws no elbows, and love is not constantly jockeying for position.

Love does not push to the front. Love does not exalt itself. Love does not grab hold of the bicycle pump of various carnal achievements in order to inflate its own name (1 Cor. 8:1). Love does not fluff out its feathers.

RISE ABOVE OFFENSE

> [Charity] doth not behave itself unseemly, seeketh not her own, is not easily provoked, thinketh no evil (1 Cor. 13:5)

We are taking care to work slowly through Paul's description of what love is like. We have noted that this is a superb description of what *Jesus* is like, and what we should be like in imitation of Him. In other words, this description of love is not an abstract and impersonal super-law, but is rather a description of personal characteristics we acquire in the process of personal imitation.

Love does not behave in an unseemly way. The ESV renders this as "rude," and the New King James says it does not "behave rudely."

Watching out for old number one is not what love does. There is a normal self-interest, which Scripture simply assumes (Lev. 19:18; Eph. 5:29), but love uses this as a standard to help us understand how to love others. Your own self-interest should be used as a standard in attaining the goal of loving others. Your own self-interest is not to be the goal itself. The sin described here is in *seeking* your own, making that your priority.

Love rises above affronts and insults. "The vexation of a fool is known at once, but the prudent ignores an insult" (Prov. 12:16, ESV). "The discretion of a man deferreth his anger; and it is his glory to pass over a transgression" (Prov. 19:11). Love is not rude itself, and love knows how to handle the rudeness of others. Good thing.

The phrase "thinketh no evil" refers to resentments. If you find yourself reviewing past conversations with others, muttering to yourself as you work through them, then this is a danger sign. Bitterness is a root, and roots gather nutrients. When the root springs up, many are defiled (Heb. 12:15).

LOVE AND TRUTH LINK ARMS

> [Charity] rejoiceth not in iniquity, but rejoiceth in the truth (1 Cor. 13:6)

This verse comes right to the point. There is one verb, used twice. Charity does not rejoice in one thing, and does rejoice in another. Though it is the same root verb, there is a distinction. Love does not rejoice in unrighteousness (*adikia*), but does rejoice in the truth (*aletheia*). The rejoicing in the first instance is *chairo* and in the second *synchairo*. Love does not rejoice in unrighteousness or iniquity, but love rejoices *together with* the truth. Love and truth are partners in joy.

The common dichotomy that pits love and truth against one another as though they were adversaries is either a verbal slander or an enacted slander. In the verbal slander, someone dismisses someone who is standing for the truth as necessarily unloving, or dismisses someone who is full of love as some kind of a doctrinal compromiser.

The enacted slander happens when the dichotomy is assumed, and the person chooses which one he wants to adopt. He stands for truth, and blows all errorists away with his machine gun of *thruppa thruppa* theology. Or he picks love, which in his mind is an amorphous gas that fills the room with sweet and sticky acceptance. Whichever way it goes, this kind of behavior makes the task of the verbal slanderer much easier, because all he has to do is say *see*?

So what does love do? Love refuses to have any joy in iniquity. Love refuses to celebrate an ungodly or perverse wedding, for example. Love refuses to lift a glass of joy. Love will be accused of many things for this, and the central charge will be that this posture is unloving. This is because people are defining love out of the wrong dictionary. In the famous love chapter, love refuses to rejoice in unrighteousness. Not only so, but love links arms with the truth, and they rejoice together.

NO THEOLOGICAL SCHADENFREUDE

> [Charity] beareth all things, believeth all things, hopeth all things, endureth all things. (1 Cor. 13:7)

In this verse, we see that love does four things. Two of them are active, and two are responsive. In the middle of Paul's thought, love believes all things and it hopes all things. This faith and this hope operate in tandem. "Believes all things" does not refer to gullibility, but rather refers to a non-cynical attitude. Love wants it to go in a positive direction, and does not want a crash so that it may indulge in a little theological *schadenfreude*, watching the triumph of total depravity once more.

It is striking that this is not a rose-colored glasses thing because this same charity bears all things, and endures all things. Love puts up with a lot, but does not do so in a way that makes it stop believing all things and hoping all things. This means that the "bearing" and the "enduring" are not done while muttering under the breath. The faith and hope are carrying a load, and the carrying of the load is not done in a way as to become grievous.

WHICH QUESTION IS IT?

> Charity never faileth: but whether there be prophecies, they shall fail; whether there be tongues, they shall cease; whether there be knowledge, it shall vanish away. For we know in part, and we prophesy in part. But when that which is perfect is come, then that which is in part shall be done away. (1 Cor. 13:8–10)

Love is never going to go out of style. There will never be a circumstance when love, when being like God, is inappropriate or unhelpful. Gifts can be put to a bad use, but fruit is what it is. The gifts that Paul has in mind here are the gifts of prophesying, the gift of tongues, and the gift of supernatural knowledge.

Even prior to the point where prophecy, tongues, and knowledge "fail," they are partial gifts, even in their prime. That which is partial is going to come to the place where it is entirely supplanted.

There are two main views concerning that which is "perfect." Is this speaking of the time when the perfect revelation of Scripture is complete and the canon is closed? Is that what Paul means by perfect here? Or is it an eschatological statement, saying that prophecy, tongues, and the gift of knowledge will "fail" when the resurrection occurs? I would tell you which one it is except for the fact that I, like the apostle here, know in part.

But in a remarkable display of even-handedness, I will simply point out that verse 12 ("face to face, even as I am known") sounds eschatological, and that the discussion of failing gifts in verse 8 sounds like they are already starting to fail, and a statement in verse 10 that prophecy will be done away with in Heaven seems odd. Who ever thought that the spiritual gifts would be operative in the resurrection? "Will we need prophets after the Bible is complete?" seems like a reasonable and pertinent question. Whether we will need prophets in the throne room of God seems like an absurdity.

PIECEMEAL REVELATION

> When I was a child, I spake as a child, I understood as a child, I thought as a child: but when I became a man, I put away childish things. For now we see through a glass, darkly; but then face to face: now I know in part; but then shall I know even as also I am known. And now abideth faith, hope, charity, these three; but the greatest of these is charity. (1 Cor. 13:11–13)

In the previous verses, we were considering whether knowing in part or prophesying in part referred to the time of the old covenant or to the time prior to the eschaton. Is the arrival of the "perfect" to be understood as the completion of the canon, or as the resurrection of the dead? We now come to the place where I come down on the question—albeit gingerly.

When images are used in Scripture, one of our first questions should concern how that image is used in other places in Scripture—and not what associations with that image might arise in our minds, for whatever reason.

The time prior to the "perfect" is described as the time of speaking and understanding in childish ways. This is not an image the Bible uses for our mortal lives, but is an image used for the time of God's children under the old covenant. "Wherefore the law was our schoolmaster to bring us unto Christ, that we might be justified by faith. But after that faith is come, we are no longer under a schoolmaster" (Gal. 3:24–25).

Paul describes the process of "becoming a man" as one, which if it is not quite completed, is at least started. "When I *became* a man." While "face to face" has an eschatological feel to it, the whole idea of knowing in part appears to apply to the time of the old covenant, as contrasted with the fullness of knowledge in the time of the New Testament:

> Of which salvation the prophets have inquired and searched diligently, who prophesied of the grace that should come unto you: Searching what, or what manner of time the Spirit of Christ which was in them did signify, when it testified beforehand the sufferings of Christ, and the glory that should follow. Unto

> whom it was revealed, that not unto themselves, but unto us they did minister the things, which are now reported unto you by them that have preached the gospel unto you with the Holy Ghost sent down from heaven; which things the angels desire to look into. (1 Pet. 1:10–12)

The knowledge of the older covenant was certainly a piecemeal affair, but when the Scriptures speak of the coming of the Christ, the note of completion is struck. "God, who at sundry times and in divers manners spake in time past unto the fathers by the prophets, Hath in these last days spoken unto us by his Son, whom he hath appointed heir of all things, by whom also he made the worlds" (Heb. 1:1–2).

Taking all this together, I take "the perfect" as God's gift of the canon of Scripture, *and all that this gift entails throughout all of Church history,* up to the culmination of all things. But this will require further explanation.

CHAPTER 14

THE TESTIMONY OF JESUS

> Follow after charity, and desire spiritual gifts, but rather that ye may prophesy. (1 Cor. 14:1)

The justly famous thirteenth chapter of Corinthians has firmly established the ranking of the fruit of the Spirit over the gifts of the Spirit. Out of faith, hope, and love, the greatest is love, and in his description of the fruit of the Spirit elsewhere, he lists love in the first place (Gal. 5:22). We saw this same truth earlier in this book. The Corinthians were gifted with every spiritual gift (1 Cor. 1:7), but that did not make them spiritual men (1 Cor. 3:1).

Having established this, he then turns to give us a ranking of the spiritual gifts themselves. Just as the fruit of the

Spirit and the gifts of the Spirit are not equal, so also the gifts of the Spirit are not equal. That is why he says here that they are to pursue love in the first instance, and after that they are to desire the spiritual gifts. Once they have turned to the gifts, the gift to be valued above all the others is the gift of prophecy.

What is it to prophesy? The testimony of Jesus is the spirit of prophecy (Rev. 19:10), and so to speak the Word of God faithfully, in such a way as to turn everyone to Jesus, is the spirit of prophecy. That spirit can come upon a man directly, as it did the prophets of old, or it can be given to a man ministerially, as he speaks authoritatively from the Scriptures.

THE PRINCIPAL VOWEL

> For he that speaketh in an unknown tongue speaketh not unto men, but unto God: for no man understandeth him; howbeit in the spirit he speaketh mysteries. (1 Cor. 14:2)

The gift of tongues is an exercise in mystery. A man speaking in tongues is a man who is speaking mysteries in his spirit. It is a mystery because the language is unknown to those present, and unknown to him. Because he is speaking to God, we know that God understands him. This means that the language is unknown, not that it is unknowable. It is an unknown tongue, which is not the same thing as gibberish.

When the disciples spoke in tongues at Pentecost, it happened that many foreign speakers were present in Jerusalem because of the festival. What Paul says here about tongue-speaking Corinth was not the case in Jerusalem. They began speaking in other tongues (*glossa*, Acts 2:4), and when a crowd gathered, they heard them speaking in their own languages (*dialektos*, Acts 2:6). We get the word dialect from that word. They were speaking in known languages.

The saints in Corinth were doing the same thing, but the languages were not known to anyone on the premises—we will learn what the point of *that* was a bit later in the chapter.

Now the fact that no one else in the worship service knew the point of what was being said is used by Paul as an argument against speaking in tongues in a service, unless it was interpreted (v. 13), and then with two or three people at the most doing it (v. 27). And not to belabor the point, the fact that the tongues were required to be interpreted meant that they *could* be interpreted. This was an unknown language, not an unknowable language.

So whether it was offered in the tongues of men or of angels, the prayers were made up of verbs, nouns, adjectives, and adverbs, with a defined syntax and grammar. It was not made up of groans too deep for words, because groaning is not language. It was not made up of jumbled syllables, with the *ah* sound making the principle vowel.

THE POINT OF PROPHECY

> But he that prophesieth speaketh unto men to edification, and exhortation, and comfort. He that speaketh in an unknown tongue edifieth himself; but he that

> prophesieth edifieth the church. I would that ye all spake with tongues, but rather that ye prophesied: for greater is he that prophesieth than he that speaketh with tongues, except he interpret, that the church may receive edifying. (1 Cor. 14:3–5)

The three elements of prophecy mentioned here are *edification, exhortation,* and *comfort*. This can happen when the prophesying is fresh revelation, as when Agabus spoke under the power of the Spirit, and it can also happen when the Holy Spirit empowers a man who is speaking expositionally from the text. In the former instance, the Spirit is giving new words, and in the latter He is keeping the preacher close to the words. In both instances, He is anointing the words. This identification of preaching with the gift of prophecy was common among the Puritans. For example, William Perkins wrote a book on preaching that was called *The Art of Prophecy*.

Aside from that use of terms, it is undeniable that in a modern healthy church, the three consequences of prophecy described here are the three consequences of good preaching—edification, exhortation, and comfort. Every preacher ought to aim for that, every time.

When someone speaks in a tongue, he himself is edified while no one else is. Tongues-speaking closes in on itself. The man who prophesies edifies everyone. Paul wishes that everyone could speaking in tongues, but more than that, he wishes that they could all prophesy. This is because prophecy is greater than speaking in tongues, unless an interpretation of tongues accompanies it, so that the

Church may be edified. This is the reason why I believe that tongues + interpretation = prophecy. A man who speaks in tongues is not just speaking his thoughts in a language he never acquired naturally. He is speaking God's thoughts, such that when the tongues are interpreted, it is the equivalent of prophecy. And so, Paul argues, in the congregation, why not just cut out the middle man?

PRIVATE EDIFICATION KEPT PRIVATE

> Now, brethren, if I come unto you speaking with tongues, what shall I profit you, except I shall speak to you either by revelation, or by knowledge, or by prophesying, or by doctrine? (1 Cor. 14:6)

Paul allows that speaking in tongues in private is an edifying activity. A man by himself can edify himself by speaking in tongues (v. 4). He may be ministered to in the Spirit because he is the only one in the room. But if there are others in the room, then their edification is only possible if there is *content*.

So, Paul says, if I come to you speaking in tongues, there is no profit in it. The only way there is profit is if content is given by one of three supernatural methods—revelation, knowledge, or prophesying—or by opening the Bible and teaching expositionally, which is doctrine.

Tongues-speaking in a group (even when it is the *genuine* gift of tongues) has no point of edification. There is one good thing that can come from it, as we will see later in this chapter, but if love for your brother is your goal, tongues-speaking in the congregation is to be discouraged.

TANGLED BLATTS

> And even things without life giving sound, whether pipe or harp, except they give a distinction in the sounds, how shall it be known what is piped or harped? For if the trumpet give an uncertain sound, who shall prepare himself to the battle? So likewise ye, except ye utter by the tongue words easy to be understood, how shall it be known what is spoken? for ye shall speak into the air. (1 Cor. 14:7–9)

Paul's argument here is *a fortiori*, a "how much more" argument. A melody cannot be made out apart from a distinction of notes, whether from a pipe or harp. And if a trumpet gives a series of tangled blasts, how will the troops know to get ready for battle? Unless there is distinction in the notes, the whole operation is just a disturbance in the air. In the same way, speaking in an unknown tongue apart from interpretation is just so much noise.

Therefore, in a Christian worship service, clarity and ease of understanding are to be prized. We are to stand opposed to anything that gets in the way of such understanding, even if that something is edifying to this person or that one individually. The body needs to be able to say *amen*.

BABEL AND PENTECOST

> There are, it may be, so many kinds of voices in the world, and none of them is without signification. Therefore if I know not the meaning of the voice, I shall be unto him that speaketh a barbarian, and he that speaketh shall be a barbarian unto me. (1 Cor. 14:10–11)

The miracle at Pentecost was a reversal of Babel, which meant that it was a *unifying* miracle. When God confused the tongues at Babel, the result was that men scattered, divided by their different languages. When God gave different languages at Pentecost, the intent was to move men in the opposite direction, to gather them all to Christ. At Babel, the different languages *scattered*. At Pentecost, the different languages *gathered*. They all heard, in their own tongues, "the wonderful works of God" being declared (Acts 2:11).

God has set the direction, and so our worship services should continue to move in that same direction. There are many voices in the world and all of them, Paul says, have specific signification. There is a meaning *there*, but if I don't know the meaning, what effect does that have? It has the effect of making the speaker a barbarian to the listener, and the listener a barbarian to the speaker. But God's purpose in the Church is to make us all members of the same household, the *same* holy nation (1 Pet. 2:9). We are not supposed to be foreigners to one another.

The word barbarian came from this idea of what alien chatter sounds like. When someone is a foreigner talking away aimlessly in my presence, I am going to tag him with an onomatopoeic label—they sound like they are saying nothing other than *bar bar bar bar*. And so, Paul says, don't do that to your brothers in church. And if you withhold from your brother the signification of what you have said, that is exactly what you are doing. You are exiling your brother, who ought to live right next door to your meaning, and you are exiling him to a distant and barbarous land.

When you do this in church, you are introducing the tongues of Babel, and not the tongues of Pentecost.

ESSENTIAL TRANSLATION

> Even so ye, forasmuch as ye are zealous of spiritual gifts, seek that ye may excel to the edifying of the church. Wherefore let him that speaketh in an unknown tongue pray that he may interpret. For if I pray in an unknown tongue, my spirit prayeth, but my understanding is unfruitful. What is it then? I will pray with the spirit, and I will pray with the understanding also: I will sing with the spirit, and I will sing with the understanding also. Else when thou shalt bless with the spirit, how shall he that occupieth the room of the unlearned say Amen at thy giving of thanks, seeing he understandeth not what thou sayest? For thou verily givest thanks well, but the other is not edified. (1 Cor. 14:12–17)

When it comes to the public meeting of the Church, the apostle Paul privileges the mind over the heart. This is not the same thing as privileging the intellect over love because the reason he is doing it is because he wants us to excel in the edifying of the Church (v. 12). The Corinthians were zealous for spiritual gifts, but he wants them to press on beyond that—with the edifying of the body in mind. A man who speaks in tongues should (as far as public worship is concerned) pray for the gift of translation (v. 13). Genuine tongues that are untranslated are therefore excluded from public worship. How much more would untranslatable sounds be excluded?

Praying in tongues is a blessing to the spirit, but not a blessing for the mind. As far as the mind is concerned, the whole thing is "unfruitful" (v. 14). Why choose? Paul says that he will pray in the spirit, and he will pray with his understanding as well (v. 15). If he does not do this, then someone who is ungifted or unlearned is in no position to say amen when the whole thing is over—which means that it must not be done (v. 16). You had a good time, but your brother was not edified (v. 17). What was the point?

We can see here a distinction between an emotional "blessing" and real edification. As the proverb goes, nothing dries more quickly than a tear. You can have all kinds of sensations, but when the sensation is passed, nothing is different. But when you build an edifice, when the project is done, the building is still there. That is what it means to be edified—the listener is built up, and changed from that point on. It is like adding a wing to your house. When you are done, the wing remains.

When the sermon series is completed, the congregation is transformed. It is like taking a journey—with a good map. When you get there, you have arrived somewhere. Speaking in tongues without true translation is like running in place.

STRAIGHT TO THE MEANING

> I thank my God, I speak with tongues more than ye all: Yet in the church I had rather speak five words with my understanding, that by my voice I might teach others also, than ten thousand words in an unknown tongue. (1 Cor. 14:18–19)

Paul distinguished praying in tongues for private edification from speaking in tongues in the assembly. He prays in tongues himself more than anybody, but in the Church he would rather speak five intelligible words than ten thousand words that are unknown to the rest of the people there. As we will see a few verses down, unintelligible speaking in church is a sign of God's judgment, not of His blessing. And if you fix that problem by translating what is said, you remove the element of judgment, but you have not removed the middle man. Why not just go straight to the interpretation? Why say something in church that nobody understands, then translate it, when you could just go straight to the meaningful talk?

TONGUES AS PENDING JUDGMENT

> Brethren, be not children in understanding: howbeit in malice be ye children, but in understanding be men. In the law it is written, With men of other tongues and other lips will I speak unto this people; and yet for all that will they not hear me, saith the Lord. Wherefore tongues are for a sign, not to them that believe, but to them that believe not: but prophesying serveth not for them that believe not, but for them which believe. (1 Cor. 14:20–22)

We now come to a place in the New Testament where it is really important to let the Testaments speak to one another. Paul starts by saying that we must not be childish in our thinking, but instead we should be mature. When it comes to malice we should *not* be mature, but in our theology we are called to maturity.

With this exhortation, Paul then quotes Isaiah 28, and cites it as his reason for encouraging them to speak intelligibly in their worship services. The context of Isaiah's warning is a context of judicial blindness, where Isaiah's warnings to the hard-hearted were all *yammer yammer yammer*.

> For with stammering lips and another tongue Will he speak to this people. To whom he said, This is the rest wherewith ye may cause the weary to rest; And this is the refreshing: yet they would not hear. But the word of the Lord was unto them Precept upon precept, precept upon precept; Line upon line, line upon line; Here a little, and there a little; That they might go, and fall backward, and be broken, And snared, and taken (Isaiah 28:11–13).

This is the passage Paul quotes when he is explaining why tongues is a sign (of *judgment*) on unbelievers. Isaiah taught them plainly, but they taunted him in return, mocking his simplistic teaching—line on line, precept on precept, sing-songy ABCing to the widdle Sunday School kids. Very well then, Isaiah says, if you treat the plain Word of God as gibberish, what you will get is gibberish. You don't listen to God when the prophet speaks, and so maybe you will understand it when your streets are full of Babylonian soldiers speaking a strange language. The end result is that they go and fall backward, are broken, snared and captured.

The same thing is promised in the law.

"The LORD shall bring a nation against thee from far, from the end of the earth, as swift as the eagle flieth; a nation whose tongue thou shalt not understand" (Dt. 28:49).

Tongues-speaking was therefore given as a sign of judgment. When the streets of Jerusalem were filled with the praises of God in multiple languages, this was a great blessing to those who were speaking those praises, along with those who heard them and entered into the praise. But it was simultaneously (and more importantly) a sign of judgment on the residents of Jerusalem who did not know what was going on. Those who accused them of drunkenness were being handed over to the judgment of God, a precursor to the Latin-speaking soldiers who would be on them within a generation. It is not a good thing.

Tongues are a sign of pending military judgment, and they were an ominous sign given to the obdurate and unbelieving. So why should such a practice be emphasized *inside* a Christian worship service? Prophecy—*intelligibility*—is for the community of faith. Why? Because we are not under condemnation, not under judgment.

TONGUES AS THE BACK OF OUR HAND

> If therefore the whole church be come together into one place, and all speak with tongues, and there come in those that are unlearned, or unbelievers, will they not say that ye are mad? But if all prophesy, and there come in one that believeth not, or one unlearned, he is convinced of all, he is judged of all: And thus are the secrets of his heart made manifest; and so falling down on his face he will worship God, and report that God is in you of a truth. (1 Cor. 14:23–25)

Paul has just finished telling us that to have a bunch of people chattering in a language that you don't understand is represented by Isaiah as a sign of judgment. He then moves on into application. If an unbeliever or an untutored person comes into your assembly, you should want the service to be edifying to him. But if everybody is speaking in tongues, the ungifted or unbelieving will simply dismiss you as being crazy. However, this dismissal would indicate that he is under judgment—as we see with the people who dismissed the Christians on Pentecost as being drunk. But Paul does say that for the believers to pray in tongues in church together is a provocation—and that is not our calling.

On the other hand, if the words spoken in the service are words of intelligible prophecy, then the unbeliever comes under the judgment of his own conscience, which is the way we avoid coming under the judgment of God. The secrets of his heart are laid bare by intelligible speech, and it causes him to confess that God is indeed present.

This is why an assembly of Christians all speaking together in an unintelligible way is simply a way of telling non-Christians to go to Hell. And while a worship service is not structured in order to cater to non-believers, it should anticipate their presence, and not place needless obstacles in front of them.

UNAMBIGUOUS INSTRUCTION

> How is it then, brethren? when ye come together, every one of you hath a psalm, hath a doctrine, hath a tongue, hath a revelation, hath an interpretation. Let all things be done unto edifying. If any man speak in an unknown

> tongue, let it be by two, or at the most by three, and that by course; and let one interpret. But if there be no interpreter, let him keep silence in the church; and let him speak to himself, and to God. (1 Cor. 14:26–28)

When the body gathers together, those with different gifts bring different things. One man has a psalm to sing, another man has a teaching, yet another has an utterance in a tongue, and a fourth and fifth man have a revelation and an interpretation. The principle is not that everyone gets to present what they have brought. Rather, the principle is that the body as a whole must be edified and built up. If the man who brings a tongue has an unknown tongue (that is, unknown to the congregation), then Paul sets down an explicit and defined rule. No more than two or three may present; they must go in order, one at a time; and everything that is spoken in an unknown tongue must be translated. If no interpreter is available, then the person with an unknown tongue must keep all the good stuff to himself, praying silently to God.

If this is the rule for genuine languages, miraculously acquired, how much more does it need to be the rule for jumbled up syllables? Those utterances which have a meaning must have that meaning rendered to the congregation. Those utterances which have no meaning at all cannot be so rendered, and so are prohibited.

WHEN THE SPIRIT SAYS TO PUT A SOCK IN IT

> Let the prophets speak two or three, and let the other judge. If any thing be revealed to another that sitteth

> by, let the first hold his peace. For ye may all prophesy one by one, that all may learn, and all may be comforted. And the spirits of the prophets are subject to the prophets. For God is not the author of confusion, but of peace, as in all churches of the saints. (1 Cor. 14:29–33)

Paul has already taught us that no more than two or three people can speak in tongues in the course of a worship service, and, if they do, then the words they speak must be interpreted. This implies that they need to go one at a time so that the words can be made out distinctly, and translated for the congregation. Some might want to represent this as a view of mine, in which I am seeking to quench the Spirit. It is actually the view of the Spirit, working through Paul, in order to quench us. Quenching ego-babbling is not the same thing as quenching the Spirit.

The same principle applies to any words of prophecy that are given. Two, or at the most three, may speak words that the Spirit inspires. The first principle noted here is that the prophets must be accountable for what they say. The others sit to judge and review what is said. No one gets to speak for God on their own authority. The second principle is that courtesy and deference apply even here. When a word comes to another prophet, the first prophet gives way. Spiritual inspiration does not bring in bedlam. One at a time, with three messages at the most. The result is that everyone learns, everyone profits. The result is that all are comforted. If any are tempted to resist this word because "inspiration cannot be denied," Paul says no.

That's not right. The spirits of the prophets are subject to the prophets, meaning that it's possible to put a sock in it. Consider that each prophet is capable of restraining himself, and each prophet is to be subject to the other prophets. The alternative to this is disobedience, which would result in confusion instead of peace. And the Spirit's work is to create order and peace, as in all the churches of the saints, and not disorder and chaos.

NOT A FLAT PROHIBITION

> Let your women keep silence in the churches: for it is not permitted unto them to speak; but they are commanded to be under obedience, as also saith the law. And if they will learn any thing, let them ask their husbands at home: for it is a shame for women to speak in the church. What? came the word of God out from you? or came it unto you only? (1 Cor. 14:34–36)

Paul has been addressing the use of spiritual gifts in the Church, but his real subject was the need for decorum and order in their worship services. And so here, when he shifts to the question of how their women are to behave in church, he is not really changing the subject.

The prohibition of verse 34 appears to be a flat prohibition, but this is only if we forget what was laid out a few chapters earlier. There Paul required any women in the service who prayed or who prophesied to do so in a manner that showed tangible respect to their husbands (1 Cor. 11:5, 10). Now in order to be able to show respect to your husband by *how* you pray or prophesy in church, it is necessary to be *allowed* to pray or prophesy there. It further means that this prohibition here is contextualized—women are to be "under obedience," as the law required. An instance of what a disorderly speaking might look like is then given—an impromptu Q&A breaks out, for example.

If anyone is prepared to dispute any of this—and we have *lots* of people like that in our day—Paul wants to know if they are the source of the Word of God, or if they were the only ones who received it. Since the answer to both rhetorical questions is no, then we see the Pauline refutation of modern feminism long before it arose.

DECENT AND ORDERLY

> If any man think himself to be a prophet, or spiritual, let him acknowledge that the things that I write unto you are the commandments of the Lord. But if any man be ignorant, let him be ignorant. Wherefore, brethren, covet to prophesy, and forbid not to speak with tongues. Let all things be done decently and in order. (1 Cor. 14:37–40)

Paul has set down the standards of decorum in worship. These standards apply as much to the spiritually gifted as to anyone else. In fact, here Paul makes clear that they apply *especially* to the spiritually gifted. If a man is a prophet or otherwise quite spiritual, he might be tempted to think that these celestial impulses of his trump the apostolic parameters. If a man thinks he is a prophet or spiritual, then let him prove it by obeying the words that the Spirit inspired. It is no good at all when men claim to be driven by the wind of the Spirit as they sail into direct disobedience of the Spirit. Letting the Spirit quench us is not quenching the Spirit.

If someone is still disposed to argue the point, Paul simply relegates him to his ignorance. Paul finishes the thought by saying that prophecy should be earnestly sought, and that tongues ought not to be forbidden. It is worth mentioning again that while tongues are legal tender, counterfeit tongues—being counterfeit—are not legal tender. To refuse to accept a counterfeit bill is not a denial of legal tender laws, but rather a support of them. To deny *yamayama* tongues is not the same thing as forbidding to speak with tongues.

The basic principle is then stated again. A Christian worship service ought to be decent and orderly. God is to be worshiped with reverence and godly awe.

CHAPTER 15

PERSEVERE IN WHAT?

> Moreover, brethren, I declare unto you the gospel which I preached unto you, which also ye have received, and wherein ye stand; By which also ye are saved, if ye keep in memory what I preached unto you, unless ye have believed in vain. (1 Cor. 15:1–2)

Paul now comes to his great summary of gospel truth. He declares to them as brothers the gospel that he had previously preached to them. Their response to this preaching was two-fold—they had received what he had declared, and they had taken their stand in what he had said. This gospel—preached and received—was a gospel that would save them, provided they kept what he had said in memory. If they had not kept this gospel in memory, then their belief would have been in vain.

I am not saved from drowning by having had a lifejacket on once. I am saved from drowning—if I am in the water—by putting on a lifejacket and by keeping it on. This is why we hold to the perseverance and preservation of the saints, which is not exactly the same thing as "once saved, always saved." Of course, if someone is truly once saved, then they are truly always saved. That is true enough, as far as it goes. But there is a category that Paul knew about—believers who had believed "in vain"—who would fit very nicely in the modern category of someone who got saved at a revival once and who has been cavorting with the devil since then. We believe that the elect, once regenerate, will in fact persevere to the end. But they will, by God's grace, persevere in holiness to the end.

AN OBJECTIVE GOSPEL

> For I delivered unto you first of all that which I also received, how that Christ died for our sins according to the scriptures; And that he was buried, and that he rose again the third day according to the scriptures: And that he was seen of Cephas, then of the twelve: After that, he was seen of above five hundred brethren at once; of whom the greater part remain unto this present, but some are fallen asleep. After that, he was seen of James; then of all the apostles. (1 Cor. 15:3–7)

The gospel is something that occurs outside of us, independent of us. For all those reading these words, the gospel was enacted many centuries before any of us were born. This being the case, as it was in the first century, the gospel spreads by means of being "delivered." Paul here outlines the objective content of what it was that he received and then in turn delivered to the Corinthians.

The first is that Christ died for our sins. The second is that He did so in fulfillment of the Scriptures. The third is that He was buried. The fourth is that He rose again on the third day. The fifth is that this also was in accordance with the Scriptures. The sixth is that He was seen by a succession of witnesses, beginning with Peter and working down to James, with hundreds of witnesses involved.

The chapter began with Paul saying that the Corinthians were to continue to believe this message, to stand in it, and to hold it in memory. That was the appropriate response to this gospel; this is the gospel for which that was the appropriate response.

This then is the content of the gospel that must be faithfully preached. Christ died as a sin substitute, He died as a *predicted* sin substitute, He was in the grave for three days, meaning that He was dead beyond all question, He rose on the third day as predicted by the prophets, and He was seen alive after that by hundreds of people.

This is the message that will be announced and declared by faithful preachers until the end of the world, and this is the message that lazy preachers instinctively shirk, and the message that dishonest preachers always try to circumvent.

UNTIMELY BORN

> And last of all he was seen of me also, as of one born out of due time. For I am the least of the apostles, that am not meet to be called an apostle, because I persecuted the church of God. But by the grace of God I am what I am: and his grace which was bestowed upon me was not in vain; but I laboured more abundantly than they all: yet not I, but the grace of God which was with me. Therefore whether it were I or they, so we preach, and so ye believed. (1 Cor. 15:8–11)

Here we have one of those brief autobiographical snippets that we find in Paul's letters from time to time. Paul acknowledges that his vision of the resurrected Lord was an untimely one. For one thing, it occurred after the Ascension. Paul is not ashamed to say that as far as the other apostles were concerned, he brought up the rear. He was the least of the apostles, and he knows that he did not deserve to be numbered among them because he had been a persecutor of the Church of God.

Nevertheless, God's grace had reached him, and he could confess that this was just the way it was. The grace that God had bestowed on him was not a fruitless grace, but Paul had wound up doing more than all the rest. If the other apostles had begun running when the starter's pistol went off, Paul didn't start running until much later. Nevertheless, he started running eventually, and he passed the others up. At the same time, Paul is careful to note that this was not his doing—had it been left up to *him*, he would have been still persecuting the Church. The reason he was able to do this is that the grace of God given to him enabled it. But, whoever it was, the other apostles or Paul, they all preached the same message, and the Corinthians had all believed this message.

AS FUTILE AS THAT

> Now if Christ be preached that he rose from the dead, how say some among you that there is no resurrection of the dead? But if there be no resurrection of the dead, then is Christ not risen: And if Christ be not risen, then is our preaching vain, and your faith is also vain. (1 Cor. 15:12–14)

Given that the fundamental Christian proclamation is that Jesus came out of the tomb on the third day, how is it that some people in a Christian congregation were maintaining that there is no resurrection of the dead? They appear to be maintaining this about a future general resurrection, but Paul pushes the logic of their position out to the end. If there is no resurrection of the dead at the end of history, then there certainly was no resurrection of the dead in Jesus in the middle of history. And if Jesus was not raised in the middle of history, then our preaching is as vain as that of an Episcopalian bishop, and our faith is as futile as that of a congregation of mainline Presbyterians who got their liberal on.

> Yea, and we are found false witnesses of God; because we have testified of God that he raised up Christ:

> whom he raised not up, if so be that the dead rise not. For if the dead rise not, then is not Christ raised: And if Christ be not raised, your faith is vain; ye are yet in your sins. (1 Cor. 15:15–17)

If the dead are not to be raised at the end of history, then Christ could not have been raised in the middle of history. And if there is no resurrection, the Christian faith is vanity. Moreover, Paul continues, if the dead are not raised, then those who testified that God had raised the dead in Christ are guilty of bearing false witness on behalf of God. If the dead are not raised, then God could not have raised the dead. And if the dead are not raised in Christ, then Christian faith is vain, and all Christians are still in their sins. Deliverance from sin is dependent upon deliverance from the dead.

One other important point needs to be made about this passage. Throughout, Paul is assuming the absolute authority of logic. For his apostolic argument, he is dependent upon the authority of right reason. If the dead are not raised, then Christ, being dead, could not have been raised. If P, then Q. P, and so therefore Q. This is *modus ponens*, and therefore valid.

If right reason is not a reflection of the absolute and holy nature of God, then we are still in our sins.

A PITIABLE LOT

> Then they also which are fallen asleep in Christ are perished. If in this life only we have hope in Christ, we are of all men most miserable. (1 Cor. 15:18–19)

If the dead are not raised, then those who have died in Christ are dead and gone. If the dead are not raised, then those who have fallen asleep in Christ have simply perished. If our hope in Christ is only a "this life" thing, then Christians truly are a pitiable lot. We, of all men, are most to be pitied. We are miserable, because we are consoling ourselves in our current miseries with a future glory that will never happen.

Paul says elsewhere that our current sufferings are not worth comparing to the glory that will be revealed in us. But, of course, this only makes sense if that future glory really is revealed in us. If nothing of the sort is going to happen, if the dead are not raised, then we are letting far too many opportunities for pleasure pass us by.

TWO ADAMS

> But now is Christ risen from the dead, and become the firstfruits of them that slept. For since by man came death, by man came also the resurrection of the dead. For as in Adam all die, even so in Christ shall all be made alive. (1 Cor. 15:20–22)

From the time of Adam on down, the saints of God had been gathered to their fathers. They had fallen asleep. They had returned to the dust. Christ descended to death, just as they had, but after a brief time in the grave, He returned to life again. Paul says here that He did this as the firstfruits of those who slept. Those who slept represented a huge amount of seed in the ground, and the Lord Jesus came back from the dead as the harbinger of what was to come.

It was fitting that a man would bring about the resurrection of the dead because it was a man who had brought about the problem of death in the first place. What Paul says here makes an implicit comparison between Adam and Christ, a comparison he makes explicit in the next breath. All men die because they are in Adam, and in the same way, and on the same principles, everyone who is in Christ will be made alive.

ENEMIES SUBDUED

> But every man in his own order: Christ the firstfruits; afterward they that are Christ's at his coming. Then cometh the end, when he shall have delivered up the kingdom to God, even the Father; when he shall have put down all rule and all authority and power. For he must reign, till he hath put all enemies under his feet. (1 Cor. 15:23–25)

The resurrection of the dead is a stupendous event, but it is also an *ordered* one. Every man is raised in the proper order, at the right time. The great event from the end of history is inaugurated in the middle of history. So Christ was raised first, and He was raised first as the firstfruits. The second wave of the resurrection will happen to those who belong to Christ, and it will happen to them when He comes again. So at the Second Coming we have the completion of the resurrection.

After the resurrection is completed, the end comes. The end will be characterized by Christ turning over, delivering up, His kingdom to God the Father. Christ is reigning now, and during the course of His reign He progressively subdues all those who set themselves as His adversaries. Over the course of history, as He has been doing for two thousand years now, He puts down all rule, all authority, and all power. His reign will extend as long as there are adversaries still to subdue. He is at the right hand of God the Father, and He must remain there until all His enemies are made His footstool. He must reign until all His enemies are put under His feet. This means that all the enemies of Christ, with the one exception of death, will be subdued to Him prior to His coming.

THE LAST ENEMY

> The last enemy that shall be destroyed is death. (1 Cor. 15:26)

In the verse just prior to this one we are told that Christ must reign as He progressively puts down all opposition to His rule. All rule and authority and power is being made subject to Him, and in this verse we see His triumph over the last and greatest enemy, which is death. On a personal note, this was the verse I tripped over when I became a postmillennialist. Some might say I tripped over it and hit my head, but here was my thinking on it.

In the more common views of Christ's reign, death is the *first* enemy to be destroyed. Human history goes along doing its thing until the Second Coming dramatically interrupts it. The dead are raised, and then comes the millennium (if you are premill) or the eternal state (if you are amill). But in both cases, death is the *first* enemy to go down. In this scenario, however, death goes down after all rule, authority, and power—with the assumption being that this is all rule, authority, and power that are opposed to Christ—has been defeated.

This means that our task, prior to the Second Coming, is through the gospel to be casting down imaginations, to be casting down every high thing that sets itself up against the knowledge of God, and to bring every thought captive to the obedience of Christ. The lion will lie down with the lamb, children will play with cobras, tornados will be diverted from their courses, and Congress will start doing good things. A man considered by his neighbors as accursed will die when he is one hundred. And after all this, with so many wonderful things accomplished, and the earth being as full of the knowledge of the Lord as the waters cover the sea, God will give the signal for the final trump, and death will be destroyed. Death and Hades will be thrown in the lake of fire.

ALL THINGS UNDER HIS FEET

> For he hath put all things under his feet. But when he saith all things are put under him, it is manifest that he is excepted, which did put all things under him. And when all things shall be subdued unto him, then shall the Son also himself be subject unto him that put all things under him, that God may be all in all. (1 Cor. 15:27–28)

This section begins with a quotation from Psalm 8:6, and the citation is applied to Christ. But if we look at Psalm 8 generally, and see how it is quoted in Hebrews, we know that the psalm is about mankind and, as the New Testament teaches us, about the new mankind in Christ. This treatment needs to be quoted at length.

> For unto the angels hath he not put in subjection the world to come, whereof we speak. But one in a certain place testified, saying, What is man, that thou art mindful of him? or the son of man, that thou visitest him? Thou madest him a little lower than the angels; thou crownedst him with glory and honour, and didst set him over the works of thy hands: Thou hast put all things in subjection under his feet. For in that he put all in subjection under him, he left nothing that is not put under him. But now we see not yet all things put under him. But we see Jesus, who was made a little lower than the angels for the suffering of death, crowned with glory and honour; that he by the grace of God should taste death for every man. (Heb. 2:5–9)

The world to come is not subjected to angels, but rather to man—even though the psalmist wonders at how kind God has been to man. Man was initially lower than the angels, but has now been promoted past the angels. All things on earth in principle have therefore been subjected to man, but it has to be man in Christ. This happens gradually—we do not yet see all things subject to man. But we do see Jesus, made lower than the angels for a time, but now exalted to the right hand of the Father. Because Jesus has been exalted in this way, we know that all enemies of Christ will be gradually subdued through the power of the gospel, from tornados to thistles, from cancer to crabgrass.

Putting it all together, this means that everything will be brought under the dominion of mankind, but it must be mankind *in Christ*. Apart from Christ, we can only make things worse.

So Christ has been seated at the right hand of the Father, and there He will remain until all his enemies are His footstool (Ps. 110:1). The one exception is the last standing enemy of death, which will be overthrown at Christ's coming in the general resurrection of the dead. Circling back around to our passage in 1 Corinthians, everything is subjected to Christ, with the obvious exception of the one who is subjecting everything to Christ—which is the Father—and so it will be that the entire cosmos will be subjected to Jesus, and He will be subjected to His Father. Why? So that God may be all in everything.

BAPTISM FOR THE DEAD

> Else what shall they do which are baptized for the dead, if the dead rise not at all? why are they then baptized for the dead? (1 Cor. 15:29)

This now brings us to a cryptic argument that Paul advances in favor of the resurrection, an argument that he advances in his famous aside about baptism for the dead. There are (at least) several ways to take this.

First, the heretical group in Corinth that was disputing the resurrection of the dead (and who made this section of the letter necessary) could have been a group that was also practicing baptism for the dead. Paul doesn't say "we" are baptized for the dead. He says that "they" are. And so

Paul's mild rejoinder to them is this—what kind of sense does that make? If the dead are not raised, then why bother getting baptized for them?

A second view is that advanced by R.L. Dabney, which is that this "baptism" refers to the ritual purification undertaken by someone who had recently buried someone. This is referred to in Numbers 19:11–13, and we know from Mark 7:4 and Hebrews 9:10 that these ritual washings were called baptisms. If there is no resurrection, then why all the Hebraic fuss over burials and cleansing from burials? In this understanding, the "they" who still do this are Jewish Christians who were allowed to continue their ancient practices (although not for justification) so long as the Temple still stood.

This second view has the advantage of not constructing an imaginary world from a few passing comments. In addition, the second view limits itself to the raw material of scriptural possibilities.

CHRIST OR COCAINE

> And why stand we in jeopardy every hour? I protest by your rejoicing which I have in Christ Jesus our Lord, I die daily. If after the manner of men I have fought with beasts at Ephesus, what advantageth it me, if the dead rise not? let us eat and drink; for to morrow we die. (1 Cor. 15:30–32)

Paul then advances another argument for the resurrection of Jesus. The apostles were witnesses of the resurrection of

Jesus, and they understood that resurrection to be a guarantee of their own resurrection. It would therefore make no sense for them to establish a fraudulent faith that did nothing but jeopardize their health and safety if they knew that the dead were not raised.

By putting this argument forward, Paul is confirming a standard argument for the resurrection of Jesus, which is the fearlessness of the apostles—in contrast to their behavior prior to the crucifixion—in proclaiming that resurrection. The apostles had all seen the resurrected Jesus, and their subsequent behavior makes no sense unless they had seen the resurrected Jesus.

Now, the identity of the wild beasts of Ephesus has been a matter of some discussion. To take it as the kind of amphitheater spectacle that later Christians had to face would be anachronistic, although it would add a little dash and danger to Paul's already eventful life. However fun, that also leaves us with the problem of explaining how Paul got away. The best explanation in my mind is to say that Paul was speaking metaphorically about the human opposition he encountered in that great city.

Still, Paul is in danger every hour. Every knock on the door could be a raid. Paul avows, with his right hand on his pride in the Corinthians, that he dies every day. This is the meaning of taking up your cross daily, and following Jesus. Why would Paul have fought the way he did at Ephesus if the dead are not raised? He is very blunt about it. If there is no resurrection, then the only sensible option is to party on the lip of the abyss. In the Pauline logic, it is either Christ or cocaine.

VIRTUE AS TEAM SPORT

> Be not deceived: evil communications corrupt good manners. Awake to righteousness, and sin not; for some have not the knowledge of God: I speak this to your shame. (1 Cor. 15:33–34)

The word rendered here as communications is *homilia*, which in other translations is rendered as company. Bad or evil company corrupts good customs, morals, or habits. The word there for manners is *ethos*. Another way of putting this is that moral stupidity is contagious, and that a person is more vulnerable to such contagion in crowds. He who walks with the wise will be wise, and a companion of fools will be destroyed (Prov. 13:20). Practical virtue is a team sport. So is vice.

Paul begins his exhortation on this point with a reminder not to "be deceived." It is very easy for us to think that our character is more impervious to outside influence than it actually is. We like to think that we can navigate the rapids of foolish company, but it turns out that our high end kayak of personal integrity is actually a leaky and cumbersome canoe.

So then wake up to righteousness, and stop sinning. Whether this admonition is obeyed or not will be seen by which crowd a person heads for—the wise or the foolish one. To head toward the people who do not know God is a demonstration that the person doing it does not know God either, and that the whole thing is shameful. Professing Christians who do this, like some of the Corinthians, need to be ashamed.

ANIMALS AND THE RESURRECTION

> But some man will say, How are the dead raised up? and with what body do they come? Thou fool, that which thou sowest is not quickened, except it die: And that which thou sowest, thou sowest not that body that shall be, but bare grain, it may chance of wheat, or of some other grain: But God giveth it a body as it hath pleased him, and to every seed his own body. All flesh is not the same flesh: but there is one kind of flesh of men, another flesh of beasts, another of fishes, and another of birds. (1 Cor. 15:35–39)

The skeptic can make no sense of resurrection. What kind of body could the dead have? The whole thing seems nonsensical. But the existence of a second body is no more marvelous in principle than the first one is. Paul rebukes the folly that cannot see that the human body is *seed*. First he notes that in order to be fruitful, a seed must die first. The second observation is that the body of the seed and the body of the plant that grows from it are strikingly different. There is continuity between them, obviously, but there is a large measure of visual discontinuity as well. So when the seed goes in the ground we should expect two things from it: one is life from death, and the second is that this life will be astonishingly different.

Paul follows the logic out. There are more kinds of seed than simply the human. Just as God creates wheat and other kinds of grain, so also He has created human-body seeds, and other body seeds. The four kinds of seed he mentions are men, animals, fish, and birds. And so will animals participate in the resurrection? Well . . . are they seed?

GLORIOUS INEQUALITY

> There are also celestial bodies, and bodies terrestrial: but the glory of the celestial is one, and the glory of the terrestrial is another. There is one glory of the sun, and another glory of the moon, and another glory of the stars: for one star differeth from another star in glory.
> (1 Cor. 15:40–41)

Paul's point here is to emphasize that God loves variations in glory, and that this love is not going away after the resurrection. If you look at the sky, you will see that celestial glory differs from terrestrial glory, although both are glorious. If you look at the sky, you will see the glory of the sun, and if you look at the night sky, you will see that the moon's glory differs from that of the sun, and the glory of the stars differs from both sun and moon. God loves inequality, but it is inequality in degrees of glory.

This is how Paul prepares us for the next thought. Man is the image and glory of God, and he is this now, and woman is the glory of man now—but in the resurrection we will see as much of a glorious transformation from our glory now and our glory then as we currently see between the sun and the stars.

YOU MAY BE A SOUL MAN NOW . . .

> So also is the resurrection of the dead. It is sown in corruption; it is raised in incorruption: It is sown in dishonour; it is raised in glory: it is sown in weakness; it is raised in power: It is sown a natural body; it is

> raised a spiritual body. There is a natural body, and there is a spiritual body. (1 Cor. 15:42–44)

Just as there are variations in glory between different objects at the same time, as between the sun and moon, so also there are variations in glory between the same object at different times. The trajectory of history is toward greater glory.

The human body now is subject to corruption, and is therefore sown in corruption. It is placed in the ground to rot. It is also placed in the ground to sprout and grow—cemeteries are, as my grandchildren put it, grave gardens. It is sown in corruption, but raised with much greater glory, the glory of incorruption. The body is dishonorable now, lacking the glory it will have. It is weak now, lacking the strength it will have, and so it will be raised in power. It is sown a soulish body; it will be raised a spiritish body.

In other words, Paul argues, our bodies now are material bodies dominated by our souls. Our bodies then will be material bodies dominated by our spirits. In all cases, we have body, soul, and spirit, but the resurrection of the dead will greatly alter the balances and ratios, and will therefore greatly alter the glory.

THE BODY AS BATTERY

> And so it is written, The first man Adam was made a living soul; the last Adam was made a quickening spirit. Howbeit that was not first which is spiritual, but that which is natural; and afterward that which

is spiritual. The first man is of the earth, earthy: the second man is the Lord from heaven. As is the earthy, such are they also that are earthy: and as is the heavenly, such are they also that are heavenly. And as we have borne the image of the earthy, we shall also bear the image of the heavenly. (1 Cor. 15:45–49)

The difference between the Adams is not that one had a body and the other did not. The first man Adam had a body dominated by his living soul; the quickening agent of the last Adam's body was the Spirit. The first Adam had a spirit, but his body was animated by his soul. The last Adam has a soul, but His body was dominated by the quickening Spirit.

The first kind of body is called natural. The second is spiritual. The first is from earth; the last is from Heaven. Those who follow Adam in his earthiness only are following him to the grave. Those who follow the heavenly Adam are a heavenly people. And all who belong to this heavenly people were recruited from the ranks of the earthy people.

So the spiritual man is not ethereal. The spiritual man is a material man—Christ rose from the dead, and appeared to His disciples in such a way as to demonstrate that He was not a spirit, not a ghost (Luke 24:39). He had flesh and bones—but they were flesh and bones that had been brought to life by the Almighty and Holy Spirit of God (Rom. 1:4).

The human body is a battery that was designed to take a much greater charge than it is now, in this fallen state, able to bear.

TRANSFORMATION IN AN INSTANT

> Now this I say, brethren, that flesh and blood cannot inherit the kingdom of God; neither doth corruption inherit incorruption. Behold, I shew you a mystery; We shall not all sleep, but we shall all be changed, In a moment, in the twinkling of an eye, at the last trump: for the trumpet shall sound, and the dead shall be raised incorruptible, and we shall be changed. (1 Cor. 15:50–52)

Paul here uses "flesh and blood" as a shorthand way of talking about our bodies in this fallen world. He is not referring to our materiality, but rather to the fact that our material bodies will decompose in the grave. After His resurrection, our Lord referred to His "flesh and bone" (Luke 24:39), dismissing forever the idea that the resurrection body is in any way ghostly or immaterial. We can see that Paul is not rejecting the material resurrection through how his parallelism works. He says that flesh and blood cannot inherit the kingdom, and then in the next phrase he says that corruption does not inherit incorruption. In this parallel setup, the kingdom of God is the incorruption. That means that the flesh and blood is the corruption.

So then, he shows us a mystery. We shall not all sleep—meaning that we shall not all die, but we will all be changed. Some who have died will be changed, and those who have not yet died will be changed. Dead bodies will put on incorruption, and dying bodies will put on incorruption. That last moment will happen in an instant, in the twinkling of an eye. The last trumpet will sound, and at that moment, that resurrection morning, the dead will come out of their graves, and they will arise out of that corruption in an incorruptible state. Those who had not yet seen corruption, but who were susceptible to it, but who had not yet died, will also be changed.

I cannot let this passage go by without mentioning here that one wit once put a copy of 1 Cor. 15:51 on a poster on the wall of the church nursery: "We shall not all sleep, but we shall all be changed."

RESURRECTION PRACTICE

> For this corruptible must put on incorruption, and this mortal must put on immortality. So when this corruptible shall have put on incorruption, and this mortal shall have put on immortality, then shall be brought to pass the saying that is written, Death is swallowed up in victory. O death, where is thy sting? O grave, where is thy victory? (1 Cor. 15:53–55)

As he leans toward the resurrection, Paul uses the language of "putting on." In fact, he uses the same verb (*endyo*) that he uses elsewhere when telling the saints to put on Christ (Rom. 13:14; Gal. 3:27). And all of this "putting on" amounts to the same thing. Putting on Christ is the same thing as putting on incorruption and immortality. And so it is that the daily acts of sanctification, the decisions to put on Christ, are all resurrection practice.

Life smothers death. The corrupt has non-corruption put over top of it. The mortal, that which dies, is buried under that which cannot die. And when this all happens, the promise given in Isaiah and Hosea will come to fruition. Isaiah states bluntly that death is swallowed up in victory (Isa. 25:8). Hosea taunts both death and the grave (Hos. 13:14).

From the first day of creation, prior to any sin or rebellion on the part of man, there were always mechanisms for translation and transition to a higher order and glory—as can be seen in the creation of Eve. Adam was put into a deep sleep, and the first bloodshed occurred when a rib was taken from Adam's side. But all of this was glorious and was attended by no corruption at all. In this sense we may say that death is the everlasting enemy, and it will be an enemy that the approaching life intends to digest fully.

FLOW LIKE A TORRENT

> The sting of death is sin; and the strength of sin is the law. But thanks be to God, which giveth us the victory through our Lord Jesus Christ. Therefore, my beloved brethren, be ye stedfast, unmoveable, always abounding in the work of the Lord, forasmuch as ye know that your labour is not in vain in the Lord. (1 Cor. 15:56–58)

Death hurts the way it does because we are sinners and deserve to die, and death is as inexorably powerful as it is because of the law of God. The law is immutable because God's character is unchanging, and death rides piggyback on the law. But through the gospel, God has devised a way to remove the sting of death and has executed a plan that overthrows the power of death—without overthrowing the law. Death is undone by resurrection, while law is not undone by resurrection—rather law is glorified and is revealed in its true character, which is that of love.

Because these things are true—because death is now a disarmed foe—Christians can give themselves to their work with a will. As beloved brothers, we are called to be steadfast and immoveable. This is a remarkable charge. We are creatures of flesh and bone, which can easily be crushed, but we are called to be steadfast and immoveable. Because Jesus rose, we are to not budge. We have set our hands to the work of the Lord, and—precisely because death is conquered—we are to abound in that work. The labors assigned to us should flow from us like a torrent.

In the light of the resurrection, we know that our toil is not in vain. It is not all going to burn, contrary to popular impressions. The wood, hay, and stubble is going to burn, but a good bit of what we do here—the gold, silver, and precious stones—is going to last forever. No good thing will ever perish forever, and no wicked thing will ever have an everlasting memorial.

CHAPTER 16

SUNDAY COLLECTION

> Now concerning the collection for the saints, as I have given order to the churches of Galatia, even so do ye. Upon the first day of the week let every one of you lay by him in store, as God hath prospered him, that there be no gatherings when I come. (1 Cor. 16:1–2)

This passage contains one of the hints in the New Testament that reveals the practice of Sunday worship in the first century. Paul brings up the matter of a collection for poverty relief among the saints, telling the Corinthians that he had given the same requirement to the churches of Galatia, and he looks for them to do the same. Paul doesn't want to start from scratch in taking up a collection, so he tells them to start collecting beforehand, week to week. He specifically says that this is to be done on the first day of the week, which is Sunday. If the money was to be "laid by" in the individual homes, then there would be no point in specifying the day. Paul wanted to prevent the need for having a big collection at church, so he required that the collection be done piecemeal, week to week, such that the gathering would be largely completed by the time he got there. In order for this to happen, the churches of Corinth (and Galatia) would need to have been meeting on the first day of the week.

PERSONAL AND ACCOUNTABLE

> And when I come, whomsoever ye shall approve by your letters, them will I send to bring your liberality unto Jerusalem. And if it be meet that I go also, they shall go with me. (1 Cor. 16:3–4)

In the previous verses, Paul had instructed the saints in Corinth to take up their collection Sunday by Sunday so that there would not have to be a last minute push. Their giving was to be part of their worship on the Lord's Day, and their giving was not to be motivated by the duress of deadlines. Christian generosity is steady and deliberate, not momentary or panicked.

When we come to his instruction here, we notice some additional principles. Paul writes ahead to have them take up their collections. He then tells them that when he arrives, they will appoint delegates to accompany their gift. The collection was for the saints in Jerusalem, and delegates from

Corinth were going to accompany the gift there regardless. If Paul did not go, they would simply take it. If Paul went to Jerusalem also, they would accompany him.

We can glean two principles from this. First, Christian generosity is personal, best delivered face to face. The Corinthians gathered the money up for the inhabitants of Jerusalem; it would therefore be best if Corinthians handed it over in person. The second principle is known accountability. Paul tells the church at Corinth that they were not simply handing the money over to him, the great apostle. He said that no, if he went to Jerusalem, he still wanted those auditors with him.

EFFECTUAL DOOR

> Now I will come unto you, when I shall pass through Macedonia: for I do pass through Macedonia. And it may be that I will abide, yea, and winter with you, that ye may bring me on my journey whithersoever I go. For I will not see you now by the way; but I trust to tarry a while with you, if the Lord permit. (1 Cor. 16:5–7)

Paul's tentative plan was to pass through Macedonia, which was northern Greece. After that he planned to go down to Achaia, where Corinth was, and spend a bit more time there. He did not want to pass through Corinth briefly, such that he merely saw them "by the way," but rather wanted to stay with them for a while. If the Lord permitted it, he hoped to spend the winter there with them. It is important to note that even the travel plans of an apostle are surrendered to the providential designs of God. He will do this if the Lord wills it.

PLANS FOR THE FUTURE

> But I will tarry at Ephesus until Pentecost. For a great door and effectual is opened unto me, and there are many adversaries. (1 Cor. 16:8–9)

After that stay in Corinth, he planned stay in Ephesus, which was eastward across the Aegean Sea. He was going to stay there until Pentecost. And then, in passing, Paul says something quite striking about why he wanted to be in Ephesus. He wanted to labor in Ephesus because a great and effectual door had been opened to him there. But at the same time he adds, "there are many adversaries." It is important to note that for Paul the presence of many adversaries does not make ineffectual work more likely. He reasons the other way. He has effectual opportunities, and his spiritual adversaries know it. They know that he will accomplish much, so they deploy great resources in an attempt to stop him. Paul's reasoning here is quite the opposite of those who reason from the existence of the obstacle to likelihood of great success. Paul reasons from the likelihood of great success to the likelihood of much opposition.

ON NOT THREATENING THE MINISTER

> Now if Timotheus come, see that he may be with you without fear: for he worketh the work of the Lord, as I also do. Let no man therefore despise him: but conduct him forth in peace, that he may come unto me: for I look for him with the brethren. As touching our brother Apollos, I greatly desired him to come unto you with

the brethren: but his will was not at all to come at this time; but he will come when he shall have convenient time. (1 Cor. 16:10–12)

Paul now gives a series of exhortations concerning two of his fellow workers in the gospel. If Timothy comes to Corinth, they are to make sure that he can work there "without fear." The reason for this is that Timothy is engaged in the work of the Lord, just as Paul was. If they received Paul, so also should they receive Timothy. What the threat to Timothy would be, what he might have to fear from them, is not mentioned. Presumably they knew what threats they might be tempted to level at a minister of the gospel working in their midst. Whatever it was, Paul told them not to do it.

Conjoined to this, and probably related to it, Paul tells them not to look down on Timothy, not to despise him. Rather, they should conduct him forth "in peace" so that he would be able to come to Paul along with some others. Paul found him quite valuable even if he knew that others might be tempted not to value him.

The subject then turns to Apollos. Paul had wanted him to come with the entourage of brothers, but he was unwilling to do so. He would come to Corinth when he had the opportunity.

PLAY THE MAN

Watch ye, stand fast in the faith, quit you like men, be strong. Let all your things be done with charity. (1 Cor. 16:13–14)

Nearing the end of this epistle, Paul gives a small burst of ethical exhortations. This cluster presents an interesting juxtaposition. The first set in verse 13 is quite martial, and then in verse 14 the "battlefield" consists of doing everything in love. One of the things that armed forces do is post sentries. The first exhortation says to "stay awake, be alert, be watchful." The second says that we are to defend our position, which we do by standing firmly in the faith. The third is an interesting stand-alone verb *andrizomai*, which literally means to "play the man." The fourth says that we are to "be strong," powerful. So then, what we are told to do here is to be alert, to stand courageously, to be masculine, and strong.

Where then do we take this? Paul says that we are to do everything in love. We can learn something about the nature of love from this. To be loving, in the sense that Paul is describing here, is something that requires alertness, a steadfastness, masculine courage, and strength. Apparently love must mean something more than sappy emotionalism.

A brief word about whether this kind of exhortation includes the women. Of course it does, but not in the spirit of "equal time" sensitivities. Among God's people the women are included covenantally. Just a few verses down, Paul says that Aquila and Priscilla send their salutation, along with the church that meets in their house. Women are clearly included in all of this, but this does not prevent Paul from using the terminology "brethren." He beseeches the brethren (v. 15), and all the brethren with him send their regards to Corinth (v. 20). This should provide us with all the guidance necessary on our use of words like "man," or the use of generic masculine pronouns. We shouldn't feel a need to do something that Scripture doesn't feel a need to do.

But many Christian men today think that we really ought to be more sensitive, and that we really ought to strive to be more inclusive. Why is this? It is actually because they are refusing to be inclusive in the way that Scripture requires. They are refusing to play the man—because whenever men play the man, they always include the women.

AS WE BOW TO EACH OTHER

> I beseech you, brethren, (ye know the house of Stephanas, that it is the firstfruits of Achaia, and that they have addicted themselves to the ministry of the saints,) That ye submit yourselves unto such, and to every one that helpeth with us, and laboureth. (1 Cor. 16:15–16)

The first household to be converted in Achaia was the household of Stephanas. But they were not simply the first converts—they had also subsequently given themselves over to the ministry of the saints. The KJV says "addicted," while the ESV says that they "devoted" themselves to service of the saints. The word for "service" here is *diakonos*, and Paul says (in an interesting gospel-twist) that the Corinthians should submit themselves to people who are like that. Servants are granted authority through their service. Paul says that anyone who is like the household of Stephanas, anyone who helps, anyone who co-labors in this way, should be honored with obedience. And so it is that in the body of Christ we serve those who serve, we submit to those who submit, we are subject to those who subject themselves, we give way to those who give way.

A COVENANTAL SYNECDOCHE

> I am glad of the coming of Stephanas and Fortunatus and Achaicus: for that which was lacking on your part they have supplied. For they have refreshed my spirit and yours: therefore acknowledge ye them that are such. (1 Cor. 16:17–18)

Paul rejoiced over the arrival of three emissaries from the Corinthian church. They filled in for the absence of the Corinthians, and they filled up what was lacking from the Corinthians. This may have included a financial gift, but in any case the three men provided a covenantal synecdoche—a part for the whole. Three men stood in for the whole church. Paul's fellowship with them was sweet, and Paul noted that they had been refreshing on both ends of their journey. They had refreshed Paul's spirit upon arriving, and they had refreshed the spirits of the Corinthians before departing. Such men should be recognized and noted. Men who have that gift are obvious, but it is still tragically easy to miss them.

MAY GOD DAMN THAT GUY

> The churches of Asia salute you. Aquila and Priscilla salute you much in the Lord, with the church that is in their house. All the brethren greet you. Greet ye one

> another with an holy kiss. The salutation of me Paul with mine own hand. If any man love not the Lord Jesus Christ, let him be Anathema Maranatha. The grace of our Lord Jesus Christ be with you. My love be with you all in Christ Jesus. Amen. (1 Cor. 16:19–24)

As Paul concludes this letter to the Corinthians, he tells them that all the churches in Asia send their greetings. These would be the churches of Asia Minor (modern day Turkey). Aquila and Priscilla add their greetings, along with the church that met in their home. This tells us that Aquila and Priscilla were probably well-to-do, capable of hosting a full church meeting in their house. All the brethren with Paul send their greetings to Corinth as well. Paul tells the Corinthians to greet one another with a holy kiss. Paul signs the letter with a flourish in his own hand, meaning that he had a secretary taking dictation up to this point. He concludes with what we would consider sentiments in tension. If any man does not love Jesus, then may God damn that guy. *Anathema* is a profound curse. Paul then issues an invitation for the Lord to come (*Maranatha*). May the grace of the Lord Jesus remain with the Corinthians. And not only does Paul want God's grace to stay with them, he wants his own love to accompany them as well. And amen to all of it.